# Glory of the Silver King

NUMBER NINETEEN
Gulf Coast Books

Sponsored by
Texas A&M University–Corpus Christi

John W. Tunnell Jr., General Editor

A list of titles in this series is available at the end of the book.

# Glory of the Silver King

## The Golden Age of Tarpon Fishing

### Hart Stilwell

*Edited and with an introduction by*
Brandon D. Shuler

*Foreword by*
Larry McKinney

TEXAS A&M UNIVERSITY PRESS ► COLLEGE STATION

This paper meets the requirements
of ANSI/NISO Z39.48–1992
(Permanence of Paper).
Binding materials have been chosen for durability.

Library of Congress Cataloging-in-Publication Data

Stilwell, Hart, 1902–1975
Glory of the silver king : the golden age of tarpon fishing / Hart Stilwell ;
edited and with an introduction by Brandon D. Shuler ;
foreword by Larry McKinney. — 1st ed.
p. cm. — (Gulf Coast books ; no. 19)
Includes index.
ISBN-13: 978-1-60344-267-1 (cloth : alk. paper)
ISBN-10: 1-60344-267-7 (cloth : alk. paper)
ISBN-13: 978-1-60344-287-9 (e-book)
ISBN-10: 1-60344-287-1 (e-book)
1. Tarpon fishing—Texas—Gulf Coast—History—20th century.
2. Tarpon fishing—Mexico—Gulf Coast—History—20th century.
3. Stilwell, Hart, 1902—-Knowledge—Tarpon fishing.   4. Saltwater fishing—
Texas—Gulf Coast—History—20th century.   5. Saltwater fishing—Mexico—Gulf
Coast—History—20th century.   6. Marine fishes—Conservation—Mexico, Gulf of.
I. Shuler, Brandon D.   II. Title.   III. Series: Gulf Coast books ; no. 19.
SH691.T2S75   2011
799.17′43097641—dc22
2010034336

# Contents

# Foreword

I first became aware of this unfinished manuscript when Texas Parks and Wildlife writer Steve Lightfoot asked me to read it and let him know what I thought about it. I am sorry to say I did not know anything about Hart Stilwell then, but I was intrigued by the title and by the fact that Steve thought I would find it interesting. And so I did. I read it straight through—I just could not put it down—and became a Stilwell admirer. I knew then that somehow this manuscript should be published. Brandon Shuler not only made that a reality but also helped me recognize just what a fascinating and underappreciated character Stilwell is. That needs correcting as well.

Even in rough form, Stilwell's manuscript hit so many buttons for me. As director of coastal fisheries for Texas Parks and Wildlife, I found the historic perspective fascinating. As an avid saltwater angler, I love a well-told fish story, and this manuscript has many. As a conservationist, I appreciated and respected Stilwell's early recognition and insight about habitat, water quality, and freshwater inflows, and the key role they play in sustaining fisheries. Finally, like many others, I have long been captured by the mystique of the silver king—tarpon. Stilwell paints a fascinating portrait of a time and fishery I can only imagine and we will never see again.

I think Stilwell could see a future when recreational fishing overwhelmed its commercial counterpart as an economic and social force, but I am not sure he imagined just what a force it would become. His writing helped energize the birth of that movement. It was the likes of Rudy Grigar and Barney Farley, to name just two Texas notables immortalized in print, who helped push the movement forward by practice. It was Stilwell's prose that opened it to everyone else. He and others mythologized the likes of Louisiana's Chandeleur Islands and the Laguna Madre's

"Eighth Pass" and built the ranks of wannabes into a real conservation force through the pages of magazines like Field & Stream, Outdoor Life, and Sports Afield.

I often stated during my tenure as fisheries director that saltwater fishing in Texas was the best on record, which was true because we had the thirty-year-long monitoring data to prove it. However, that record started in the mid-1970s when populations of red drum and spotted sea trout were laid low by the overharvest of commercial fishermen and the bycatch and trawling impacts of an overcapitalized and underregulated inshore shrimp fishery. Stilwell's manuscript adds to the anecdotal record of books and stories like Fishing Yesterday's Gulf Coast, by Barney Farley, and Plugger: Wade-Fishing the Gulf Coast, by Rudy Grigar, describing a time just before commercial fishing was introduced to the efficiencies of the diesel engine and nylon gill nets and before the adverse impacts of coastal development and pollution really made themselves felt along the coast. I admit, they clearly were the good old days. I cannot imagine and few now can remember the quantities and quality of the red drum, spotted sea trout, flounder, tarpon, and snook these men lived with and wrote about. Imagine being awakened at night by the noise of fish feeding on a school of migrating shrimp, as Stilwell was when camped on the bank of the fabled Eighth Pass of the Laguna Madre, or jumping sixty-three tarpon in a day on the Panuco River at Tampico, Mexico.

If it were not for the conservation ethic of dedicated anglers, inspired by writers like Hart Stilwell and motivated by organizations like the former Gulf Coastal Conservation Association (now the CCA), I am sure we would not be where we are today. We have recovered the red drum and spotted sea trout fisheries in Texas and much of the Gulf coast to levels that many could not imagine just a few years ago. The CCA has become an economic engine that over the last several years has added nearly a thousand jobs a year to Texas coastal economies, helped restore thousands of acres of habitat, and improved water quality for both us and the fish. It is a multibillion-dollar industry in the Gulf of Mexico.

Many challenges remain, and Stilwell saw where they would come from long before many of his day. His vision is today's reality. Modern fisheries management has gone about as far as it can through regulating bag and size limits, seasons, and even hatchery production to restore and maintain the fishery we now enjoy. Stilwell recognized that it was our degradation of the water quality, the diversion of freshwater from our estuaries, and loss of habitat to coastal development that would ultimately determine the fate of our fisheries, both commercial and recreational.

On retiring from Texas Parks and Wildlife, I have moved on to direct the Harte Research Institute (HRI) at Texas A&M–Corpus Christi. It was an opportunity to address these very issues and help take the next step in restoring the full potential of our coastal waters and the estuaries that are such an integral part of them. One of the HRI projects I have helped to initiate is developing partnerships in Mexico to restore the coastal fisheries that Hart Stilwell talks about in this manuscript. I have traveled and boated many of the places he describes therein. The only things that have not changed for the worse are the people. They are wonderful, resilient, and, despite grinding poverty in many areas, getting on with life in ways that I can only admire and wonder at. They deserve better and with a little help can achieve it.

It is our goal to help reduce the overfishing by providing alternative sources of income and food through artisanal aquaculture models and developing recreational fishing and ecotourism to take advantage of their existing water-based skills. Stilwell saw this potential as well and talked about ways to use his beloved tarpon and snook to accomplish the same end. His ideas of stocking and restoring tarpon have not proved possible and perhaps not even desirable, but his intent was on target. If HRI and the international partnerships that are being built succeed, some of what he foresaw as needed and possible will happen.

In the end it was two things that kept me reading this lost manuscript. One was the topic—tarpon, the silver king. We have lost a great resource and a source of inspiration from this part of the Gulf when the fish dwindled to the current sad state. There are many things I like about Florida (difficult for a native Texan to admit) and one of which I am jealous, and that is their access to this marvelous fish. It makes me realize what we are missing. Oh, there are still tarpon here and more than many know or will tell about. One of the great thrills of my life was when my nine-year-old hooked his first and only tarpon in Aransas Bay. He cried when it threw the lure back at us on the third jump, but he was hooked for life, just like the rest of us. Today, at sixteen, he still talks about it. I would like to see more have that opportunity.

The second reason is one that I hope you will appreciate in your reading of *Glory of the Silver King*. Hart Stilwell writes with a raw honesty and directness that one does not often see these days. It is a bit rough and when he talks about Mexican cathouses, a little uncomfortable, but if you remember when this was written, understandable. That aside, his description of fishing and his relationship with his fishing buddies and their adventures, are timeless. It made me long to have been there, but because I never will have that chance, I can only imagine it. For that, Hart Stilwell, I thank you.

Larry McKinney
Harte Research Institute

# Introduction

## FINDING HART

It was fall 2002, and an early evening red harvest moon rose in the mouth of the harbor. A landscapist, with easel and palette, could not have centered the moon more precisely than nature was doing at that moment. It was late October, and the first light norther of the season rolled in with a sea mist obscuring the brilliant white dunes of South Padre Island that, on clear evenings, glisten across the water of the lower Laguna Madre. The norther brought with it a feeling of change that accompanies late fall in deep South Texas.

In a Rio Grande Valley fall, white-wing dove are more often found on grills than in the air; buck whitetail are shedding summer velvet in preparation for the midwinter rut to come; flounder and redfish are exiting the bays to the gulf, in mass, to spawn and continue the fragile circle of life; and flocks of Redhead, Widgeon, and Blue- and Green-Winged Teal that spend the winter dodging .12-gauge shotgun blasts and roiling in the relative warmth of the winter Laguna Madre are flying in from the north in colorful waves of late fall plumage.

Steve Lightfoot, editor of *Texas Sporting Journal*; Kenny Redin, the journal's graphics and advertising guru; and Aaron Reed, who is trying to raise awareness of environmental conservation issues along the Texas coast by kayaking its length, all sat on the rear deck of my family's hunting and fishing lodge with my dad and me, enjoying the view of Port Mansfield harbor and the Gulf of Mexico beyond.

Like the season and wildlife around us, Dad and I, in the middle of a hard season of guiding, were in a transition too. The winter operation at Getaway Adventures Lodge shifts from pure fishing excursions to a combination of winged hunts, deer hunts, or even the odd excursion stalking the exotic nilgai, a beast imported in the nineteenth century by the Kings and Kenedys as a cheaper, heartier alternative to cattle.

Wintertime is best known in the lower Laguna Madre as "trophy" speckled trout time. In the gray, frigid, misty south Texas winters, trophy trout are a tarpon aficionado's wintertime release. Although the work as a guide is hard, punishing, and not one of the better-paying endeavors a man can undertake, it is something that runs in the blood—my blood. I'm in my thirties, but the strength of the Texas sun has etched itself in the corners of my eyes and on the backs of my hands. I can read the water, weather, and waves like one of the novels that lie in my boat's console. My lullaby as a child was the hum of the wind whistling through the taut strings of well-strung rods and the call of gulls and curlews digging for their dinner.

As I glance at the moonlit faces of the men around me, I feel a connection in the reverence each pays to the view rising in the mouth of the harbor. Their blood, my blood, rises and ebbs with the tides that flush and cleanse the flats.

Between Steve, Kenny, and my dad, they represent a part of a Texas heritage that, in this age of instant gratification and greed, cannot be lost. And as emerging voices of Texas wildlife conservation and outdoor journalism, Aaron and I are responsible for carrying on these stories and mores and lifestyle, just as the men sitting here that came before us did and those that came before them.

As the moon's largesse shrunk in its rising trajectory, the elder statesmen, tongues loosened by a few Coronas and Don Julio tequila, were in a yarn-telling mood. Aaron and I listened to the soft drone of wisdom and knowledge that floated on the cool air and we absorbed our coast's past.

"Bubby Brister was an icon," Steve said. "He's one of the original voices of the Texas outdoors."

"You know, Steve," my father said, "Bubby taught me how to hunt sandhill and ducks off Wallisville Road in Houston back when it was nothing but a mere gravel road out into the pine woods."

That revelation, that simple statement, "back when," says it all for the outdoorsman. Each subsequent generation gets the previous generation's "leftovers," because "back when" the seas, lakes, and rivers teemed with fish and the woods with varmint and bigger game. What the newer generation inherits is a sea assaulted by more anglers and better fishing equipment and faster boats and fewer fish.

Bubby Brister, longtime outdoor columnist for the Houston Chronicle, had befriended my paternal grandfather, an Ozark Mountains, backwoods country boy from Arkansas. They'd fish and hunt long hours together, while my dad listened and absorbed their stories.

As my dad grew older, he had me tagging along on hunts and fishing trips and absorbing conversations about the ever better "back when." On other occasions, I'd sit on the front porch stoop learning boat knots or some other boy scout arcana, while Pawpaw and my dad shared stories about Bubby and trips along an old single-lane, gravel-paved road down south to a foreign place called Arroyo City. The roll of the Rs and the soft landing of the -yo felt exotic and dangerous on my tongue. It was also the first time I heard the name "Hart Stilwell" in conversation. Maybe it was the "Hart" that caught my attention. It wasn't common. It wasn't the odd effeminate names like Lesley and Connie and Allison I heard when male, East Texas family members came around for Thanksgiving and Christmas dinners.

No. Hart, to a child, was the personification of that beating orb in your chest that, from the sidelines, dad always screamed to have a lot more of when I stepped to home plate or climbed onto the swim blocks.

As Steve and dad and Kenny traded Brister stories, Aaron and I turned our conversation to the tarpon season that was quickly coming to a close with the cooling weather. I tried to follow Aaron's story about his Port Aransas tarpon, but in the background I overheard Steve telling dad about a lost manuscript.

"What?" I asked, interrupting Aaron's fish tale. "What manuscript?"

"Well," Steve said, "we were doing some research in Hart Stilwell's archives at the Wittliff Collections, and we came across an unpublished manuscript."

"What's it called?" my dad asked.

Steve leaned forward. You could read the excitement on his face, and he suddenly looked uncomfortable, wringing his hands one moment, putting them in his lap the next, and finally lacing the fingers together. "Glory of the Silver King," he said.

Steve commenced to melt back into the wooden Adirondack chair that supported his Texas-sized six-foot-three frame. It was if he had unleashed the secrets of the Zapruder film, revealing to us the true conspirators of JFK's assassination, and the weight of the unveiled truth left him visibly lighter. He looked around, meeting us each eye to eye, and with a wry, dimpled grin smiled back at us through an ever-chilling evening.

Anyone who has battled a silver king can easily excuse Steve's enthusiasm. Tarpon hold—damn, even command—a special place in an angler's heart. The dramatic runs. The dogged persistence not to give up before the angler. The gravity-defying leaps. The "nice sound" of rattling gills that Hart Stilwell describes in "Glory of the Silver King." They are uniquely tarpon.

It's why, when inexplicably the damn fish simply spits the hook and swims away after a two-hour battle, you, with forearms burning, fingers curling into a fist from the constant pressure applied to hold the rod, and body drenched with sweat, cast right back into the fray.

It's why we travel eight hours through exotic back rivers like the Tamesi and Panuco and Monkey or through the Nicaraguan rainforest braving children-stealing–sized mosquitoes and Jesus Christ lizards and fer-de-lance snakes to get a peek at a silver flash of rolling tarpon.

It's a fever.

It's sleeping uncomfortably through a sticky rainforest night to the tune of a million buzzing mosquitoes accompanied by the do-wop of the howler monkey.

It's tarpon, man.

The only other words in the angler's lexicon that can even begin to challenge the word tarpon are "fish on!"

"So," I said, barely able to contain my growing excitement, "besides being about tarpon, what's it about?"

Steve stretched out his size-thirteen Crocs, those god-awful fishing shoes that seemed to be all the rage a few years ago, and laced his fingers across his stomach.

"The manuscript needs a lot of work," he sighed. "But it's basically a history of tarpon and snook fishing on the Texas coast and in northeast Mexico in the 1940s and '50s. There's nothing else like it from back then. This guy lived the rise and decline of the Texas coastal fishery."

"Can I read it?" I asked.

"Sure. I don't have a copy here, but I'll send you one once I get back to the office."

As a die-hard tarpon aficionado, I couldn't wait to get my hands on a copy of the manuscript or the finished book, which Steve said a group of investors was interested in publishing. Unfortunately, as with most alcohol-laced post-fishing promises, when Steve returned to the responsibilities of the real world, the assurance to send me the manuscript was forgotten as e-mails and phone calls vied for more pressing attention.

Previous to that 2002 evening conversation about "Glory of the Silver King," a disturbing trend was beginning to reveal itself in the gill net surveys that Texas Parks and Wildlife uses to monitor the health of estuarine fisheries. As an ardent "trophy" trout angler and one with a vested family interest in my home waters, I involved myself with the media and TPW to develop a grassroots campaign to lower the limits on the speckled trout take in the lower Laguna Madre.

The liberal catch limits of ten fish per angler per day combined with an increase in angling pressure were decimating our bay's stock. Over the previous ten-year span, Dad, our guide staff, and other concerned anglers began witnessing smaller and smaller fish and fewer numbers of "keeper" fish. The lower Laguna Madre appeared to be heading toward becoming a "back when" fishery. Although the situation was not a "fishery in collapse," as lower Laguna Madre TPW Ecosystem Leader Randy Blankinship assured everyone it wasn't, it was tenuous. A devastating winter freeze could damage the trout population in the lower Laguna Madre to such an extent that TPW might shut down trout fishing all together.

To thwart a "no fishing" zone in my Mother Lagoon, I launched the trout campaign in 2002. At the time, I was frequently appearing in regional publications like *Gulf Coast Connections*, a tiny rag of a newspaper with a small but rabid readership; David Sams's *Lonestar Outdoor News*; and a couple of Texas newspapers. Soon, though, I was receiving offers from national publications like *Shallow Water Angler* and *Salt Water Sportsman* to tell the lower Laguna Madre trout's story to a larger audience.

As I waded through the national requests and the learning experiences of managing my first environmental campaign, Steve, from *Texas Sporting Journal*, called one day and asked whether I wanted to cover the trout situation in the lower Laguna Madre for him.

"Sure," I said. "I'd love the opportunity."

"We can only pay you a couple of hundred bucks," Steve said. "If that's okay with you, of course."

Suddenly, I remembered our conversations about a "lost" Stilwell manuscript the previous year. A good angler, I know when to set the hook.

"I'll tell you what, Steve: a couple of hundred bucks and throw in that manuscript we talked about when you were down with Aaron, and we're on."

"What manuscript?" he said.

"The one about tarpon and snook by Stilwell."

"Oh! Oh, yeah," he said. "Done."

I went to work on the article and campaign. I called Dr. Larry McKinney, head of TPW Coastal Fisheries, and Robin Riechers, TPW Fisheries economist and policy specialist, to get quotes and scientific data concerning the speckled trout in the lower Laguna Madre. These phone calls and e-mails eventually led to great personal and working relationships with two of the more progressive fisheries managers TPW has seen.

I worked on the trout article, my first opus, for a couple of days until the manuscript arrived in a beat-up, blue-and-white, one-price USPS box. I tore off the perforated strip and revealed the manuscript of "Glory of the Silver King."

As pressing as the trout issue was, I admit I put the article and campaign aside for a day and dove into the story and the history of Texas tarpon and snook fishing. I was riveted. Hart knew the fever: He was infected, as I am, and he captures the mystique of the tarpon. I could see the battles with the silver king as he writes in this account of wade fishing along the sandy shore of the Rio Grande:

> Two hours, and the trail I was walking, back and forth, began getting deeper. Three hours, and I couldn't take it anymore. I got a grip on the sand with my feet and clamped down with both thumbs—on the sides of the reel spool, not on that tiny bit of line left on the reel. I guess it was pretty funny, me and that tarpon doing our tug-of-war. He would thrust with his broad tail, trying to surge forward, and I would lean way over as far as I could without falling, but I wouldn't give him an inch of line. When he stopped and sighed, maybe sticking his nose up just enough to get a breath of air, I would work on him, getting back four or five feet of line. Then another surge. The fragile, worn line held.

It is in such narratives Stilwell captures what the battle means to a tarpon angler. My longest struggle with the silver king lasted five hours on a Nicaraguan shoreline in twelve-foot seas. The battle seems never-ending, tackle may give at any moment, you're so wasted you're even wishing for the fish to break off, but you still hope this is the one that won't get away.

I plowed through the manuscript, barely setting it down, but eventually got back to my article and trout campaign. I worked the phone to legislatures, other captains, environmental groups, chambers of commerce, and anyone who would listen to the plight of the lower Laguna Madre speckled sea trout.

A year of lobbying, writing articles, and traveling to numerous TPW public comment meetings finally paid off on a cold and blustery Austin, Texas, February day. Dr. McKinney sat at the head of the table before the TPW Board of Commissioners and worked through the coastal fisheries agenda.

Coincidently, one of the agenda items, beside my belabored sea trout, was the issue of lifting the ban on Texans' rights to keep one tarpon per year. Historically, anglers could keep a tarpon for trophy reasons only if they purchased a game tag from TPW. The agenda item explored a petition for regulation change to allow anglers to keep one tarpon over eighty-seven inches, if caught, to challenge the sixty-five-year-old Texas record.

As Dr. McKinney argued for raising the moratorium on killing tarpon for sport without a trophy tag, he mentioned to the commissioners that a few TPW employees had a manuscript in their possession called "Glory of the Silver King," by Hart Stilwell. Dr. McKinney wanted to see the book in print due to its historical perspective on Texas fisheries and the slice of Texana it provided for those interested in that sort of thing.

After a short conversation about "Glory of the Silver King," the commission agenda proceeded, and the sea trout item came before the commissioners. As soon as it was raised, Chairman Peter Holt, principal owner of the San Antonio Spurs, asked whether members of the commission knew any reason why the speckled trout limits in the lower Laguna Madre should not be lowered. No one spoke, and the commission unanimously passed the measure to lower the limits, effectively saving the speckled sea trout population in the lower Laguna Madre.

As elated as I was to win my first environmental conservation campaign, burning in the background, though, was that name and manuscript again; it was as if Hart Stilwell and "Glory of the Silver King" were calling to me. In a sense I guess they were.

Flash forward a year or two. I found myself employed as a public high school teacher in deep South Texas in Hart's old stomping grounds of the lower Rio Grande River Valley. Much like Hart, I tend to lean a little to the left of the political spectrum, which is always to the chagrin of our cantankerous and conservative fathers. I thought, like Dave Atwood did in Stilwell's novel Border City, that I could make a difference in the lives of the underprivileged people of south Texas. Unfortunately, like Dave and Hart, I too learned that idealism is lost to the harsh realities of the poverty-stricken Rio Grande Valley.

My intellectual curiosity and growing national writing popularity from the success of the trout campaign, mixed with a healthy dose of disillusionment with the public education system, led me to seek an MFA in Creative Writing from the University of Texas–Pan American. I entered the program with the express purpose of learning how to write biography—Hart's biography.

Early on, one of the classes I took was with Dr. Rob Johnson, whose biography of William S. Burroughs, *The Lost Years of William S. Burroughs*, follows the pre-writing life of Burroughs during his years as a farmer in South Texas, 1946 to 1949. The text explains the complex, racially charged history of the Rio Grande Valley Burroughs had escaped to while running from a New Orleans district attorney hell-bent on placing him in jail for a minor narcotics violation. Johnson made the autobiographical content of Burroughs's fiction jump off the page.

In one Tuesday evening class, discussing the political and social makeup of 1940s south Texas, Dr. Johnson dropped the name again—Hart Stilwell.

This was the first time I had met someone outside of hunting and fishing circles that knew who Stilwell was. In fact, Johnson and I came to Stilwell from two different avenues—Johnson purely from the academic side, and me from the outdoor writing side. After class I told him I was interested in writing Stilwell's biography.

At the local Logan's Steakhouse, over drinks to discuss my Stilwell biography—which was to moonlight as my thesis—Johnson asked me how the Stilwell research was going. "Great," I said. However, as I said it, I knew that the research was not going as well as hoped. As Stilwell says in "Glory of the Silver King," "I collect memories, not things."

Although Stilwell was one of the most prolific outdoor writers of the twentieth century, with over 250 articles in *Field & Stream*, 200 in *Sports Afield*, 150 in *Outdoor Life*; numerous articles in magazines such as *Esquire*, *Parade*, *True*, *The Nation*, *The New Republic*; and with three autobiographical novels set in the lower Rio Grande Valley, he left behind not a single personal journal and only sparsely saved correspondence.

"Well, actually Dr. Johnson," I confessed, "it's not going as well as it could. This guy left no journals and few letters, and most of his publishers have either trashed his author files or no longer know who he is. I think I'm really at a crossroads here. How do I write a biography of a man that left so little?"

Dr. Johnson made a brilliant suggestion: "What about that lost manuscript you keep telling me about? The one about tarpon? You might try editing and annotating it."

The shot of Don Julio tequila present the night I first heard Steve Lightfoot mention "Glory of the Silver King" seemed to cross the cosmos of six years and find itself deposited in the fresh glass of Don Julio sitting in front of me. Was "Glory of the Silver King" really seeking me to get it out to the world?

"You know, you are the modern day Stilwell," Johnson said.

Sweating a deadline for *Outdoor Life* about the Texas Parks and Wildlife's ShareLunker Program, but wasting time drinking Don Julio and talking about the Beats and Stilwell in south Texas, somehow awakened me to the fact: Yeah, I may be the modern Hart Stilwell. I convinced myself that, yes, I was the perfect voice to get "Glory of the Silver King" edited and in print. Stilwell and I are both from the lower Rio Grande Valley. We are both Texan, altruistically driven, eco-conservation–minded liberals. Our politics, although Democratic, tend to a kind of left-leaning conservative flavor, which in the rest of the country would label us as Republicans. We both took a stance on estuarine environmental activism—in fact, Stilwell first suggested lowering the Laguna Madre speckled trout limit in a 1942 *Brownsville Herald* editorial. We also, albeit separated by a half century, write for a number of the same publications, like *Outdoor Life*, *Field & Stream*, and *Salt Water Sportsman*. We both left decent-paying day jobs to write full time, so we could pursue and fund our true passions—fishing and hunting. At the least, I owed Stilwell and "Glory of the Silver King" a look, to determine whether the manuscript was salvageable. To do that and to get the book to print began with a trip to Texas State University's Wittliff Collections in San Marcos, Texas.

The Wittliff Collections at Texas State University are a vast and veritable treasure trove of Texana writers and luminaries. Steven Davis, assistant curator and author of *Texas Literary Outlaws* and *J. Frank Dobie: A Liberated Mind*, held my hand through my first archival experience in search of a clean manuscript of "Glory of the Silver King" and other Stilwell artifacts.

Steven led me through the etiquette of digging through old letters and manuscripts. He offered me a seat and told me his coworker would bring out the collection in a few minutes. A tiny rap at the door, and there they were: three acid-free manila boxes containing multiple drafts of two unfinished book manuscripts, a handful of old magazine and newspaper clippings, and a few "lost" photographs by famed Texas and Works Progress Administration photographer Russell Lee.

I dove straight into the three drafts of "Glory of the Silver King." Steve Lightfoot's assessment was correct; my job would be taking a collection of yellowed, coffee-stained scribbles, cross-outs, and type-overs that still smelled faintly of smoke and nicotine, and putting them into publishable form. From one draft to the next, words would appear, then disappear, only to reappear in the next draft. Entire sentences would hinge on a two-letter preposition, and Stilwell obviously struggled with which one to adhere to. Entire stories would appear in one draft, then be gone in the next, or mysteriously move from chapter to chapter. But like the lure of the tarpon that called Stilwell and me to travel the length of the Gulf and Central America, the desire to get this manuscript together and into print was overwhelming. It was my job to solve the mystery and build it into a readable draft.

As I read through the three drafts, focusing my attention on the most complete version, the original pull and excitement with which I first read "Glory of the Silver King" returned. I was no longer only a fishing guide. The long hours I'd spent earning my master's in literature (I'd bailed on the MFA program to study literature under Dr. Johnson) and reading seventeenth-century satire, literary theory, post-colonial literature, and a smattering of literary genres forced me to read the text with a rejuvenated verve and a new eye for literary detail. I realized I held something special in my hands: something that not only fishermen and outdoorsmen would enjoy, but also readers who valued history, particularly lost portions of Texas coastal outdoors history.

My task had begun.

Hart Stilwell's journey toward "Glory of the Silver King" began with his birth in Yoakum, Texas, in May 1902. The family moved to the Rio Grande Valley when he was two and settled in the Harlingen area. It is here he began fishing and hunting, first for family sustenance and later for pleasure. He attended the University of Texas at Austin as a journalism major from 1919 to 1924. After graduating, he returned to the Rio Grande Valley and worked as a reporter for the *Brownsville Herald*, where he ultimately became the editor from 1942 to 1944. However, frustrated with the political wrangling of publishers and South Texas political bosses like Jim Wells and R. B. Creager, Stilwell left the newspaper business to become a freelance writer and soon wrote three autobiographical novels: *Border City*

(1945), *Uncovered Wagon* (1947), and *Campus Town* (1950). Although *Uncovered Wagon* did earn a mention in A. C. Greene's *The 50+ Best Books on Texas*, these are not the books for which Stilwell is best known.

While working as a journalist, Stilwell was quietly becoming one of Texas's best-versed outdoorsmen, from fishing to hunting. During the '40s and '50s, Stilwell served as a fishing or hunting guide to John Dos Passos, Russell Lee, J. Frank Dobie, and Texas governor Jimmy Allred. Stilwell even concedes he could have been considered a commercial fisherman because he supplemented his "fishing habit with his writing." He longed to find a way to parlay his love of the outdoors with his gift of writing. After leaving the *Brownsville Herald* in 1944, he did just that, writing the two books that ultimately forged his legacy, *Hunting and Fishing in Texas* and *Fishing in Mexico*.

*Hunting and Fishing in Texas* and *Fishing in Mexico* are essential travelogues for outdoor enthusiasts hunting and fishing in the respective locales. They are written in the straightforward narrative prose indicative of Stilwell's writing for journals like *Outdoor Life*, *Field & Stream*, and *Outdoors*. What most makes these texts important, though, is the development of Stilwell's conservation ethic, which strengthened as he got older. The writing of both books created a moral dilemma in Stilwell. He confesses remorse for exposing the people of Mexico and their fisheries to the "Nordic Horde." J. Frank Dobie tries to assuage Stilwell's concerns in a letter dated 8 December 1948:

> Of course your book will go far towards ruining some of the people and some of the fishing waters that you tell about. You are bound to cause an influx of Americans, but I guess that is all right.

As he traveled to these locales at different times, such as the trip to Carmen, Stilwell found the effects of fishing pressure and the subsequent overfishing placed on the local fisheries were destroying the stocks. Stilwell realized, as my dad, myself, and others noticed about the speckled trout in the lower Laguna Madre, that fisheries cannot withstand abject, unmitigated pressure. He responded to Dobie on 13 December 1948:

> Glad you liked the fishing book. It seems to be getting pretty good reviews . . . I share your views about what will happen to the Mexicans—and what is happening now. But that is one thing none of us

can check. . . . At any rate, I hope I don't bring them too much grief because of my own writing.

Stilwell was one of the first to argue that if steps were not placed in motion to protect ocean populations, then pressured fisheries would soon become "back when" fishing holes. The idea of his beloved tarpon becoming a "back when" fishery was the impetus behind the writing of "Glory of the Silver King." Unfortunately, he died before he could get it to print.

Hart Stilwell's *Glory of the Silver King* is not up to the standards of a modern biological study, but it is a wonderful fishing tale with prescient advice on how to save the tarpon and our oceans. *Glory of the Silver King* is a warning of the effects of misguided wildlife management, if you will. And although Stilwell's biology may be outdated at times and some of his ideas, such as warming the Great Lakes, may sound a little kooky, most of his ideas and his passion are in the right place.

However, Stilwell's brand of "environmental" message artfully masks itself through the first part of "Glory of the Silver King." Stilwell reflects on the glory days of fishing behind the dredges that dug the Brownsville Ship Channel. Or how, on one fishing trip, *Field & Stream* editor Ray Holland and he had to draw straws with their fishing companions to determine "who had to go catch dinner" in the middle of a hurricane that had trapped them on the beach of the Mexican Laguna Madre.

But as adventurous as his fishing tales are, Stilwell, as the book progresses, steadily builds his message against humans' impact on our wildlife and environment and offers prescient advice and suggestions to stem the intrusive tide of our encroachment into the domain of wilderness.

*Glory of the Silver King* suggests that one of the greatest threats facing our coastal fisheries is the lack of shrimp in our bays and estuaries caused by commercial fishing and shrimping. In his fishing trilogy, *Fishing in Mexico*, *Glory of the Silver King*, and *Hunting and Fishing in Texas*, Stilwell attacks the great numbers of commercial shrimpers who troll coastal bays and accuses them of effectively wiping out the quality of shrimp in the ocean and therefore negatively affecting fish populations. Stilwell remembered the day when only five Gulf shrimp comprised a pound. To remedy the situation, Stilwell suggests instituting a shrimpers' license buy-back program to limit the number of shrimpers in the Gulf and Texas bays. He wrote these words in the years between 1968 and 1971. Texas Parks & Wildlife did not begin the shrimp license buy-back program until 1995, almost thirty years after Stilwell first suggested it. And it wasn't until 2000, when Dr. Larry McKinney persuaded TPW for additional saltwater stamp monies from the sales of fishing licenses, that the program really took off.

What *Glory of the Silver King* is depends upon the reader. For a fisherman, this is the time for the tarpon to usurp that big, old blue marlin immortalized by Papa Hemingway in *The Old Man and the Sea*. For the environmentalist, it is a microcosmic study of the waning population of our oceans through the eyes and experience of one man as he witnesses the effects of a lack of coordinated fishery management on pristine fisheries during his lifetime. And for the conservationist, it is another in a long line of stories that start "back when." For all of us, *Glory of the Silver King* is a reminder that it takes all kinds of people and experiences to save and properly manage our natural resources.

*Glory of the Silver King* was, much as the tarpon, a difficult catch to land and bring to the boat. The drafts, which exist in four varying levels of completion, are disjointed and were initially an enigma to decipher. Stilwell made a number of starts and stops in the writing and shifted content from chapter to chapter as he wrote, making the task of determining his narrative intent difficult.

The Wittliff Collections houses three of the four manuscripts, and two of these were crammed into a small, acid-free folder in no cohesive order. The fourth and most complete draft, from which most of this version of *Glory of the Silver King* originates, I obtained from Stilwell's grandson, Benjamin Acosta-Hughes. The pagination of each document varied wildly as Stilwell worked to put the narrative into a sequence that shifted the point of view from the fishing tale to a warning against overfishing and natural resource exploitation.

Stilwell's career as a journalist and magazine writer was responsible for the additional element of short, choppy paragraphs to his writing style. Where this type of writing is indicative of news-style, hard-boiled writing, it also appears that Stilwell used these short paragraphs as part of his writing process. The first two manuscripts are composed of short one- to two-sentence paragraphs and contain an overwhelming use of dashes and fragments, as if he were simply getting the idea on paper. Each subsequent draft fleshed out ideas in varying levels of detail and completion, until the fourth draft, which apparently was hastily put together and sent to Alfred A. Knopf by Stilwell's wife, Anne Stilwell, after his death in 1975. This is suggested because the fourth manuscript has the return address referenced to her in 1976, rather than Hart.

In editing the original manuscripts, I created from these short paragraphs an extended narrative paragraph that matches the paragraph style of excerpts from the manuscript published in *Field & Stream* and Stilwell's other fishing books, *Hunting and Fishing in Texas* and *Fishing in Mexico*.

The first ten chapters of the fourth manuscript contain the most complete and succinct writing in *Glory of the Silver King* but are also where most of the paragraph condensing occurs. The last eight chapters, however, were incomplete and required the most organizing and reconstructing on my part. Chapters 4 and 11 represent the greatest amount of chopping and rearranging on my part to help with narrative flow. I used all four draft copies to give the story the most complete and readable form possible.

The most challenging editorial exercise appeared in Chapter 16: "Farewell to the Rio Grande." Stilwell had six versions of the chapter in the manuscript collection, and for good reason. "Farewell to the Rio Grande" represents Stilwell's cathartic farewell not only to the Rio Grande, but to fishing as well. Each of the six versions vacillated between dripping sentimentality, which Hart was often guilty of, and frustration with attempts to capture the beauty of what the outdoor world meant to him. In "Farewell to the Rio Grande," Stilwell attempts to balance the end of the fishing tale of "Glory of the Silver King" with the environmental message he presents in Chapters 17 and 18. This juggling act made editing Chapter 16 difficult because I wanted to capture the remorse of the aging Hart Stilwell at the end of his active lifestyle, while faithfully arranging the narrative to lead into the final chapters' powerful environmental message. I believe I got as close as I could to Hart's original intent.

Beyond structural and line editing for clarity's sake, at no point in the editing did the editor change ideas or make judicious changes of context that the modern-day reader may find offensive. In several points of the narrative, Stilwell uses the term "wetback" to describe Mexican laborers who have illegally entered the United States. Taken from another author, this could be construed as a derogatory and debasing moniker; however, the reader must understand that Stilwell, in the early 1940s–50s, was a major supporter of the Mexican American and illegal-alien civil rights movement on the Rio Grande border (see Stilwell's novel *Border City*). He used his position as editor of the *Brownsville Herald* as a soapbox to get these stories of discrimination, at least in some truncated version, to the readers. When Stilwell uses the term, he is speaking from a time when "wetback" was not politically incorrect. I left Hart's "wetbacks" and occasional misogynistic statements intact to give the reader the true flavor of his vernacular and authorial mien.

Throughout *Glory of the Silver King*, in Stilwell's prose, most often married to the hard-boiled style of the newspaper editor he once was, a certain edge of aged-tempered softness creeps into the story. We can, however, forgive Stilwell for the encroaching softness in his narrative; it stems from his reminiscences on a life once lived in the company of other adventurous and tough men in wild and untamed waters while he relates the story of the glory days of tarpon fishing in Texas. As Stilwell writes *Glory of the Silver King*, it becomes obvious that the memories he captures on paper are his "last" fishing trips. At one point, he reminds the reader that not all promised fishing trips will come true, and in the end the only promise we all keep is the one with death.

From the pages of *Glory of the Silver King*, Stilwell is reluctant to relinquish his faith in his fellow human to stop the decline of tarpon and protect our environmental domain. Stilwell's belief in humankind's ability to do the right thing, though, does not deter him from warning that if something is not done to stem the effects of people on the environment, we will never experience the world as he did. In the narrative, Stilwell attempts to pass on the beauty of his experiences and bequeath us the gifts of the silver king in all its glory. Yet Stilwell did this knowing this was his last book. So, in reverence and respect for the greatest fish alive and for one of the most interesting characters in Texas letters, I can only hope I did Stilwell's words justice.

Brandon Shuler

# Prologue

## AND IN THE BEGINNING . . .

The year was 1934 and it was not a very good year. It was the depth of the Big Depression . . . the year was lousy. I was standing on the flat, sandy bank of the Rio Grande near its mouth. The Rio Grande flowed into the Gulf of Mexico then. It does now—on those rare occasions when it flows. Much of the same water moves back and forth with the tides. Occasionally, a sandbar forms across the mouth, then the river is landlocked. And a motorist might cross into a foreign land without being aware of it—an illegally entered alien.

Water was flowing that day back in 1934—quite a nice current. Mullet by the tens of thousands were moving upstream to feed on plankton and other goodies moving down with the current. And tarpon by the thousands were cruising near the mouth of the river, grazing on the mullet. This might be termed cannibalism twice removed, since tarpon and mullet are distant cousins. But cannibalism doesn't bother fish any more than it does human beings—the objective is survival.

Out in front of me in the moderately clear water the big fish were showing. Silver kings, we call them. The jumbo herring, the king-size sardine. The tarpon were rolling, as fishermen say in describing the motion of this fish when it comes to the surface to gulp a big breath of what was once referred to as fresh air. Tarpon are an old, old species. They have functional, although somewhat rudimentary lungs—funny little reddish strips inside the air bladder. This is the gadget that helps fish maintain a certain water level without effort. But it is more than a mere balance to a tarpon. It is a lung, and periodically he must give it some air.[1]

If a tarpon is staying in one spot, letting a current bring the food to him, he turns sideways at the surface, showing a broad, silvery side that glistens in the sunlight. As he turns to go back down after getting the breath of air, he is likely to slap the surface of the water with his tail—it is a nice sound. If the fish shows some other way, he is either feeding at the surface or traveling. I'll talk about that later.

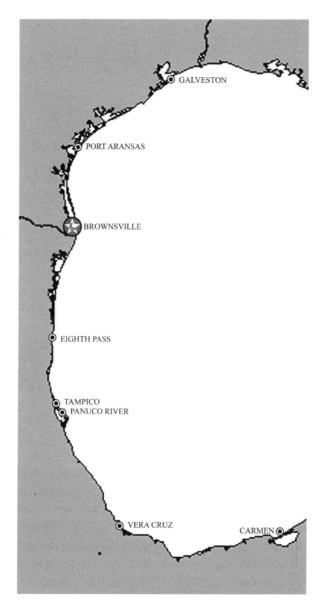

I had never seen a tarpon before that day, even though I had lived at Brownsville, only thirty miles from the mouth of the Rio Grande as the crow is supposed to fly but never does. The Rio Grande sure doesn't go in a straight line in that part of its delta. It throws loop on loop like a sidewinder moving across hot sand, and it is more than ninety miles from the mouth of the river to Brownsville as the river "flies."

So I was getting all set to do battle with my first tarpon—my first silver king. I smile now as I reflect on that first cast. I was using a huge surf rod, a mighty saltwater reel and a bait combination that Rube Goldberg might have dreamed up.[2] The bait was a mullet, hooked through the head from the bottom with a hook big enough to hold a small whale. Above the hook was a big swivel, and attached to that was a five-foot chunk of heavy steel leader. At the other end of the leader was another swivel, and topping off the rig was a square cork attached to the line.

It took a long, rugged rod and a hefty heave by the angler to get all that junk out into the river where the tarpon were, so the line had to be strong. Merely trying to cast that rig would have broken the far lighter lines I used later in my battles with the silver king.

I managed to get my bait combination far enough out so the current would carry it to the school of tarpon. As it neared them, I popped the cork, as fishermen say, by jerking with the rod tip. It is one of the most effective techniques in taking tarpon as well as many other species of gamefish, particularly channel bass, which we in Texas call redfish; weakfish, which we call speckled trout; and snook, which we used to call pike but now call snook.[3] Practically all pole-and-line commercial fishermen use the cork-popping technique. When you jerk, the cork goes under, making a nice plunking sound. When the cork bounces back up, it pulls the mullet upward. Gamefish down below think the mullet is making a dash for the surface, trying to escape. A big fish, even if he's not hungry, can't endure the sight of a little fish escaping.

The second time I popped the cork, a six-foot tarpon latched onto the mullet and almost yanked me into the river as it took off on a wild run. Yes, I know fish don't run—they swim. But to fishermen they run. I had tightened the star drag on the big reel so much that the tarpon got a solid pull against me, and I had trouble holding my grip on the sand. At the end of the run the tarpon burst high in the air and rattled its gills. That's what we call it—rattling gills. If you insist on precise terminology, you would say the tarpon rattled his gill flaps. And if you said that, the tarpon fishermen I know would consider you a nut of some kind.

The silver king really does a fancy job of gill rattling. He opens his mouth wide and shakes his head from side to side so fast that you see only a blur. It wasn't until years later that I learned, by studying photos, that the fish actually moves his head through an arc of 180 degrees. So in some shot I made, it seemed that the fish's neck was broken and his head dangling at right angles to his body. That's what a tarpon does in trying to turn loose when he realizes he clamped down on the wrong thing. And the noise of gill rattling is like that of giant castanets. You can hear it a quarter mile away—another very nice sound. And please don't bug me by saying that the tarpon making that "nice sound" is in pain and terror. I know that. I also know what's happening to the boxers in the ring and the football players who crack each other up. Much that man calls sport is and has been since the beginning the inflicting of pain in one way or another. I ain't trying to reform him—and I choose not to be reconstructed in my own attitudes. After all, the most vicious "sport" of all is that inflicted with words.

While my first tarpon was in the air—even before he fell heavily back to the water—I became an instant aficionado. An addict. I knew that I had found the kind of fishing worthy of dedicated effort. So for thirty years I pursued the big sardine, all the way from the Louisiana–Texas line to the southern tip of the Gulf of Mexico, where offshore waters are the Gulf of Campeche, not the Gulf of Mexico. I followed him up the big Panuco River, billed for years as the king of tarpon rivers. I went all the way to Carmen, land of iguanas and coconuts and parrots. I saw the Southern Cross there. Pretty puny sight—a big tarpon is more interesting. I followed the jumbo herring out into the open Gulf as far as he goes—to Isla de los Sabalos (Tarpon Island) offshore from Vera Cruz, Mexico.[4] I worked hundred of miles of surf, fished all the inlets I could reach, explored bays and canals and ship channels and tiny rivers where the tarpon had never before seen an artificial lure. Wherever tarpon moved, I followed.

I have battled the big fellow with all kinds of tackle, ranging from the mighty rig I used at the beginning, on through a process of evolution, winding up with something just about perfect for the job. There can never be the perfect tarpon casting rig because he comes in different sizes. Real fine light tackle for three-footers isn't worth a hoot if a six-footer takes hold, unless you're the kind of nut who wants to chase a fish, using a boat, for six hours and do ten years bragging. And gear that is perfect for the six-footers doesn't give a flashy two-footer a chance to really show what he can do. It would be real nice if an angler could put a "No Babies Allowed" sign on the plugs for the big ones and "No Adults Allowed" on plugs for the little tarpon. Real nice—if a tarpon could read and, having read, followed instructions instead of doing what human beings do. But let's get on with the story.

Actually, my thirty-year pursuit of the tarpon just about spanned the days of glory of fishing for the silver king—the rise, the peak period, and the decline. I choose not to say "decline and fall"—at least not at the moment. In fact, I tell this story in the hope that it might, in a small way, contribute to the survival of the great fish.[5] But this is not a book on ecology. Anybody who can hear or read or understand ASL (American Sign Language) knows the estuarine creatures—crustaceans, fishes, some mollusks, and so on—are in a bad way. And the tarpon is an estuarine fish: part of its life cycle is spent in brackish or fresh water. Thousands of specialists are busy trying to save those estuarine species—that is, the species that have commercial value.

I tell a fishing story.

I present here the drama of battling at close range the greatest game-fish that can be caught by casting and I get a kick out of retelling my story. Perhaps you will get some vicarious joy from a retelling of those moments of drama. You might even become interested enough to go along with me when I say that the tarpon can be saved, even though no efforts along that line are being made now.

Why?

Because he is not considered a commercial species, such as the weak-fish and flounder and striped bass and channel bass and shrimp and oysters that marine biologists are struggling to save. If the tarpon is saved, this happy event will take place as something of a byproduct of our campaign to save the creatures we eat. So I will tell my fishing story. Then in the last chapter I will put down some things I think we might do to keep this "Eagle of the Seas" from joining the dodo in serene oblivion.

I've got some ideas that might seem pretty dopey to you. For example, how about bringing the tarpon inland? If that sounds screwball, just note progress now being made in the campaign to bring the striped bass, another estuarine fish, inland. You can reasonably claim that the parallel is not valid because the tarpon is a tropical fish that cannot endure cold temperatures in our lakes. And I can counter by saying that this is not the only country on earth, and maybe the tarpon can be brought inland in tropical areas.

That's not all.

If he needs fairly warm water to survive, heat the doggone water. What's wrong with heating the Great Lakes? We spend millions doing things far dopier. Then tarpon hatcheries can be set up and man can step in and conduct the love life of the tarpon, just as he now performs the mating ritual for rainbow trout and for those striped bass being brought inland. It's a cinch the environment in this country in the year 2000 A.D. is going to be about 95 percent manmade. Why not fit the tarpon into that environment, just as we do with hand-fed deer and pen-raised quail and so on?

But let's get on with the fishing story.

People refer to horse racing as the sport of kings. I like to think of tarpon fishing as the sport of presidents.

There is at least a fragment of logic in this designation. A president-elect, Warren Gamaliel Harding, and a president, Franklin Delano Roosevelt, were responsible for calling attention of the American public to the tarpon. Few Americans knew there was such a fish before newspapers in the land flashed that famous FDR smile in a picture, with a huge, well-dead tarpon suspended beside the President. Suddenly tarpon fishing became fashionable—except among those economic bourbons who had substituted a curse on FDR for the traditional grace before meal. But Harding conducted the groundbreaking ceremony—the prelude. He went to the little Texas coastal town of Point Isabel, now called Port Isabel, back in the early 1920s, and he fished for tarpon.[1]

I have only a vague recollection of the visit because, even though Brownsville was my home, I was doing time at the University of Texas in Austin. Furthermore, I considered Harding a fatuous fake that should never have been inflicted upon the people of any nation. I do recall that the inauguration was later then than it is now, and that Harding went to Point Isabel, which is only thirty miles from Brownsville, as a guest of the late R. B. Creager, Republican boss of Texas for a quarter of a century.[2] And I recall mention of the president-elect fishing for tarpon. They sure must have moved up from Mexico early that year.[3] But—nothing is too good for a president-elect, even though he could be an incredibly dull buffoon. So Americans generally heard about the tarpon, although no grand rush to

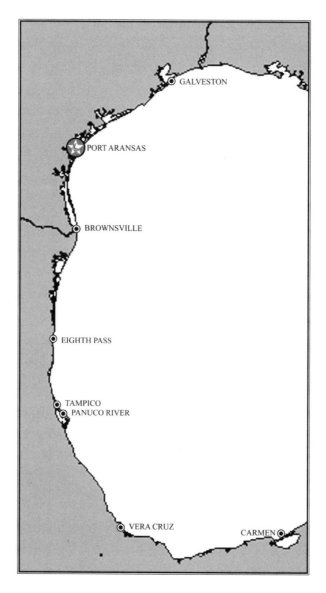

catch the fish resulted as it did after the FDR tarpon jaunt. Things changed then. Tarpon are Democrats.

It was in the middle of the Grand Depression, and people were searching for something, just anything, that would furnish a moment's relief from the dread monotony of unemployment and hunger. So when the man in that old shopworn "man stands beside dead fish" picture turned out to be the President, people looked, wondered, and reacted. At last they knew there was such a fish as the tarpon, and that he was considered some punkins among the angling elite. I doubt if a picture of Melville standing beside Moby Dick would have aroused more interest. Everybody knew there are whales. So this one is white? Who cared? So it is fictional and demonstrated strange reactions that could result only from thinking at the human level. Who cared?

So for my money, the era of glory of the silver king started that day back in the 1930s . . . I think it was 1936, but I could be off a year one way or the other. And that era of glory was of importance to me in several ways. I had just launched my long career as an outdoor writer, and editors of such magazines as Field & Stream, Outdoor Life, and Sports Afield looked with much more interest on tarpon fishing articles that I sent them. That increased interest meant more income from my fishing activity (actually, I could have been classified as a commercial fisherman), so I was able to start roaming the vast coastline of the Gulf of Mexico in pursuit of tarpon.

FDR caught his tarpon in waters at Port Aransas, on up the coast from Port Isabel. He made the trip in a ship—I think it was the presidential yacht. His trip coincided with the beginning of the once famed tarpon rodeos along the coast of Texas, and later in Mexico, particularly in the Panuco River at Tampico.[4]

Of course, tarpon fishing started long before that—way back in the previous century. In fact, I am sure that natives along rivers in tropical countries have been catching tarpon, for purposes of eating, for thousands of years. They still do along many of the rivers in Mexico. But I am talking about anglers deliberately going after tarpon for sport, not those who accidentally hooked one of the big fellows while fishing for something else and not the natives who caught tarpon on heavy hand-lines and ate the fish. In the latter part of the past century there were quite a few anglers who sought out tarpon in the shore waters and estuaries and canals of Florida and a few in Texas. But in earlier days, 99 percent of anglers were "meat fishermen," and they considered those who deliberately hung tarpon as a class of nuts.

"Why fool with a big, dangerous fish that's not fit to eat?" was the general attitude, and I loved that attitude. It meant that only a few anglers went after tarpon, and this big gamefish won't put up with crowding by anglers. He either takes off or learns how to ignore them. So let the meat fishermen have their fun in their own peculiar way, and I say "peculiar" since they can buy the same fish in the market at one-tenth the cost, a logical situation, since a commercial fisherman is ten times more efficient than an amateur.

I became a dedicated tarpon fisherman for reasons that I consider eminently sound, and they can all be lumped into one statement I have already made: The tarpon is the greatest of all gamefish that can be caught by casting a lure. Yes, I've spent time, plenty of it, struggling with other great gamefish, some far larger than tarpon. Hemingway wasn't telling me anything new in *The Old Man and the Sea*, and if the Nobel Prize judges had gone to the trouble of catching a marlin, then catching a tarpon by casting, they would have awarded Hemingway his prize, which he deserved, for some other book—*A Farewell to Arms*, or maybe *For Whom the Bell Tolls*—not for the overblown chunk of rather mushy melodrama about that old man and his marlin.[5]

Sure, I've battled marlin. If you want to fight big gamefish, you should do the same. A stirring experience. But I get an odd feeling of detachment when a marlin puts on his show, even when every flap of his tail as he maintains his position during that fantastic aerial run is telegraphed to me through the line. He's too far away—two hundred, maybe three hundred yards. I have an illusion that it's happening to somebody else and I am a mere spectator. But did you never look up at a giant silver king arched over your little cartop boat and see him glaring down at you as he rattles his gills, flinging a big plug from side to side? Do that before you low-rate the tarpon as a gamefish.

You troll for billfish, and almost all the time with live bait—which really isn't live anymore. That's okay with me. I still love to troll for marlin and sails. But you can't do any good casting for them, especially with a lure. Now and then some free sails will follow a hooked fish up to the boat, and if you let your bait down and jiggle it, you might get a strike. But it's not casting. How can you cast with a seven-foot rod and a twelve-foot leader? You can't. So you never experience that thrill of the jolt that comes when you drop a lure on a feeding tarpon, maybe thirty yards away, and he blasts at the surface and bounces instantly into the air.

Anyway, tarpon fishing as a sport for many thousands of Americans, maybe hundreds of thousands in the days of glory, began coming into its own not long after the president-elect and then the president moved into the picture, but I'd better hurry back to the mouth of the Rio Grande and do something about the tarpon I had on my line that day in 1934. It isn't fair to leave him there rattling his gills forever.

# CHAPTER 2

# The Fat Lady

"It's a fat female," said Hurt Batsell. "You've got your work cut out for you."

I wasn't paying much attention to comments—too many things happening all at once.

Hurt Batsell lives at Brownsville. He is the man who took me by the hand and led me into the world of tarpon fishing. It was pretty new to him, although he had fished for other saltwater gamefish for years. I hadn't.

I had a silver queen, not a silver king, on my line. A fat lady, as tarpon fishermen say. The female is broader in the beam and thicker than the male. She is not as likely to wear herself out lunging into the air again and again. She dogs it . . . sometimes on and on. The human female is not the only one that knows the survival value of sheer endurance.

Under ordinary circumstances I could have stopped that six-foot fat lady with the mighty gear I had. A fish does not take off in a straight line and run forever when it feels the hook and the drag of the line. It makes a run; then, if it's a tarpon, it probably tops the run off with a burst in the air, tossing in some gill rattling. When it falls back to the water, it may hesitate, sort of regrouping mentally and meditating on strategy. You go to work then, pumping and reeling to get some line back. When the tarpon takes off again, it may go in a different direction. It may even come directly at the angler, in which case it is almost certain to get slack, which makes throwing the lure easier. The fish battles that way—a run, a leap, a pause, a run in a different direction. If you can hang on, the runs become shorter and less speedy, the jumps fewer and less violent. You wear the fish down. But

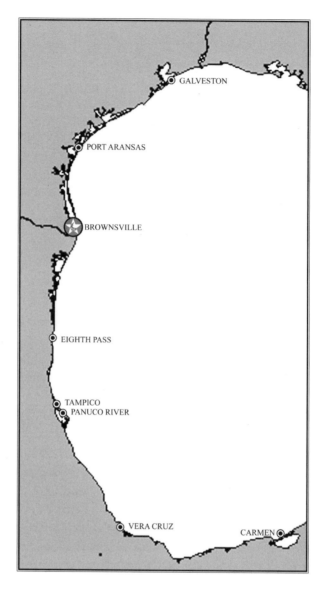

my situation was not typical. You could properly say that the point of sandy beach on which I stood, where river met gulf, was my point of no return. No sane person in possession of all his faculties would venture far beyond that point, for rollers were washing on up to the beach, and the rip tides caused by the strong river current meeting gulf waters kept washing little holes in the sandy bottom. I can swim all right. But I don't do a fancy job of it when I'm fully clothed, wearing hip boots, and hanging onto a big rod and reel with a tarpon on the end of the line taking full advantage of the current in its dash for the open sea. That's what my fat lady was doing—heading for the open sea. My only hope was to sort of nudge her out of the current and into the eddy water near shore. Then the rollers would come to my aid and rip tides might help, but that wasn't the fat lady's idea. She refused to be nudged out of the current, even though it curved a bit toward shore.

I had no place to go. I went anyway. No man abandons his first tarpon without giving it the old college try. I followed the big fish until water was up to my arm pits and small rollers were breaking over my head at times and line kept spinning off the reel faster than ever. I was vaguely aware of some shouting onshore behind me. At first, I didn't hear what was being said—too much concentration on the fat lady. Then the sand on which I was standing suddenly melted away, and all of a sudden I was hearing that sound from shore—loud and clear.

"I'm casting out—LATCH ON!" Hurt was shouting.

He had used cutting pliers to snip the steel leader just above the hook and had quickly replaced hook and mullet with a sinker weighing about the same—heavy enough for a long cast but not heavy enough to sink the cork. He had to get the mullet off because a free tarpon might take the thing as it neared me. Or, still worse, a shark might latch on. Plenty of sharks were cruising those waters a bit farther out than the tarpon. Sharks love to assemble in such spots, where they can lie in wait for a tarpon foolish enough to flip a fin in water roiled up by clash of river current and gulf. Tarpon usually ignore the sharks, and you get the impression that the sharks are ignoring the tarpon. The two swim surprisingly close to each other at times, merely cruising. Each knows exactly what he is doing. The tarpon is faster and knows it. So does the shark. But let some misfortune, such as getting fast to a fishing line, happen to the tarpon and there is likely to be a wild and bloody flurry—and the angler winds in a tarpon's head. They don't give prizes for tarpon heads.

I sort of floated for a moment when the sand washed out from under my feet, then I was on moderately firm sand again—at least temporarily. I turned and saw a cork floating right to me. Just as I latched onto it, my fat lady made a frantic run—a shark probably spotted her—and there was a popping noise as all the line ran off my reel. It broke at the knot I had tied, running the line through a little hole that makers of reels put in the reel spool for that purpose. Maybe they still do that. I wouldn't know, since I abandoned such heavy reels years ago. But that hole . . . it is without doubt the most stupid thing ever conceived by man. The line is certain to break at the sharp edge of the little hole. Otherwise it is certain to break near the leader, where it is weakest. Casting wears the line there. One way you lose all your line; the other way you save it all. Of course I should have clamped down before all the line ran off—let it break where it should. But when you're grabbing a cork with one hand and standing on floating sand, you don't think of all those things.

Batsell "landed" me by pumping and reeling much as he would have done in working in a big spent tarpon.

When I waded out onto the shore, he said, "I wouldn't try that again."

"I won't," I promised.

Such promises aren't worth any more than the ones a man makes to his wife. Your reactions when you fish for tarpon are conditioned reflexes. If the tarpon shows, you cast at him, even though he is only ten feet from your eggshell of a boat. Solemn oaths mean nothing in moments of unexpected temptation. You cast and worry later. Some pretty dopey things can happen when you do that, like the time a five-footer landed smack in Batsell's lap on its first leap right beside our little boat. So there he was shouting "Shoo! Shoo!" as though a tarpon understood chicken language, while the big fish was fluttering and banging around.

It finally "shooed."

I ran another line on my reel and assembled another rig. I moved upstream a bit from the school of tarpon and heaved my booby trap bait out far enough so the current would carry it to the fish. I hung another one, a lean, long, fiery male. The hook must have got a bite in the tarpon's funny bone, for it went nuts, spending more time in the air than in the water. It seemed to use the water only for "footing" so it could launch itself aloft once more. In a fairly short time I was able to work that one in close to shore and get a grip on the leader. As I slid the tarpon onto the sand, Batsell got a pair of pliers and took out the big hook. Then, to my astonishment, he started shoving the fish, with his feet, back toward the water.

"Hey, man! What are you doing?" I said, alarmed.

"We never kill a tarpon," he said.

"You crazy or something?! That's my first tarpon. Nobody is going to put it back in the river."

I lugged the jumbo herring home and showed it to people until the stink got so strong that I couldn't take it. Then I gave him a decent Christian burial.

# CHAPTER 3

# King of Tarpon Rivers

I am going to skip eight years and more than three hundred miles to tell you about tarpon at a different fishing hole. Then I'll go back and pick up anything that seems worth picking up. There is no rule saying I must observe chronological order in telling this story.

The place is the Panuco, which flows into the Gulf of Mexico at the city of Tampico. Although I had run into some spectacular tarpon fishing in Mexico, at and near inlets into the huge Laguna Madre of Mexico, I had not fished the Panuco. One reason was money—the depression was just winding down, largely because of the buildup for war. The second reason was the war. It was 1942 and for more than a year no tackle for sports fishermen had been made and none was going to be made for a long time. So those of us who had acquired special tackle for tarpon nursed the stuff—we were reluctant to go to the Panuco and watch the monsters there chew up our plugs and bust our lines.

Those Panuco tarpon were monsters, as proved by a world record fish that I saw when the man who caught it (I do not recall his name) proudly displayed it at the Brownsville Airport on his way back home. It was a 247-pounder, far greater than any tarpon ever caught on tackle, although I heard unverified reports now and then of 300- pounders being caught in nets.[1] The man who caught the record fish left the impression with me that all tarpon in the Panuco were giants. "It is the King of Tarpon Rivers," he said—and soon the people at Tampico, noting success of various tarpon rodeos along the Texas coast, decided to capitalize on what they had. They announced the first Tampico Tarpon Rodeo.[2]

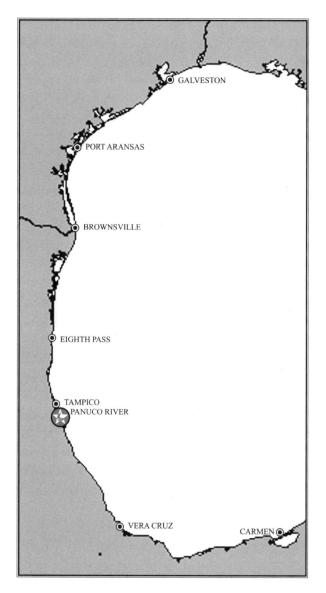

Soon afterward I got a letter from Felix Florencia, who operates a tackle store in Tampico and headed the first tarpon rodeo organization, asking me to take part in the rodeo as his guest. He had seen some magazine articles of mine about tarpon fishing and said he hoped I would write up their rodeo. I conferred with my two regular fishing companions, Hurt Batsell and Dave Young, and they agreed to go along. But they were worried about tackle, so I wrote Felix, explaining the situation.

He called me.

"You don't have to bring tackle," he said. "I've got plenty for you."

"But there will be three of us," I explained. "Also, we expect to pay all our expenses but the boat, in case you will take us out in yours."

I don't like deadheading and never have. The few times I let myself be fast-talked into a free junket, the results weren't too hot. In the first place, it really wasn't free. I never made any long trips alone, and I would arrange to pay my share of the total cost, reduced by only one deadhead. I learned early in the game that you commit yourself too deeply. Not only are you expected to get stories in magazines and newspapers, but you are bound to say only favorable things.

"I'll have tackle for all of you," Felix assured me.

"But we use lures," I said, "not mullet."

"We don't use mullet either," he said. "We use Pflueger Record spoons. Tarpon can't hurt them."

I had told him in my letter that the big ones in the Panuco were likely to crush our lures, many of which had punk, American-made hooks instead of fine Swedish hooks. So I was relieved about the plugs. And about lines, which were in scarce supply. And even more about rods. For I had a good idea what might happen to our long, one-piece, relatively light rods in those DC3 planes. I'd had a few busted when they were poked under the seats, which was the only place to put them, and there were few replacements.

Hurt and Dave and I had made the transition to moderately light casting tackle years before the junket to Tampico. We seldom trolled. And I figured we would do plenty of casting in the Panuco. I sure was disillusioned in a hurry on that idea. But when you go to another man's fishing hole, you do as he does, as I will explain later.

When we cruised out onto the broad Panuco and saw the telltale flashes of light on the water a mile upstream, I was willing to admit that it deserved its title as the "King of Tarpon Rivers." The Panuco makes the Rio Grande in its lower delta area look like a crooked drain ditch running through wasteland. The Panuco is broad, a half mile in places. The Rio Grande is so narrow at times that we used to trick suckers by betting that we could cast across it—at the mouth. The suckers always fell for the bait, for they had been watching us cast, and we weren't going halfway across. But replace that seven-eighths-ounce plug with a lead sinker the same weight, and you could throw the thing away—or at least across the Rio Grande at the mouth. And nothing was said in the bet about what object we would cast.

The Panuco is in the tropics—beautiful tropics. Bananas and papayas and palms and all manner of other lovely foliage line its banks, and there is river traffic, whereas the only water traffic in the Rio Grande were a few funny little paddle-wheel boats used during the later part of the past century to link Brownsville to the Gulf, where cargo was littered out to waiting ships. There were river launches in the Panuco, operating on schedule, carrying both passengers and freight. There were awkward-looking freight boats pushed along by one oarsman. And I say pushed, not pulled, because the man stood up and pushed on his oar handles, the way so many people do in Asia and some other parts of the world. It's easier on a man to stand and lean into oars than it is to sit and pull.

And there were dugouts and canoes of all sizes, some so tiny I was amazed to note how effectively they served their one passenger.

There was human habitation all along the stream—and along the lower delta of the Rio Grande there is nothing but scrub brush and willows. We even managed to locate a little cantina right on the river bank, and we had a fine time resting in the shade of banana plants and drinking tequila to give us strength for the next tarpon—that we didn't catch. And it sure was untouched by gringo hands. No tourist trade. The man at the little cantina wouldn't even take our U.S. coins, a few of which were left over when we changed to Mexican money. But the bartender would take one half peso— and I mean that literally. People, probably frightened by all kinds of war rumors, had hidden their metal money. There was a simple solution to the problem of change—tear a peso bill in half. Everybody went along fine with the idea, and so did we. The half peso was worth about eight cents, as I recall it, so we didn't need smaller change. Cost of replacing those torn bills became so great that the Mexican government finally worked some strategy, I don't recall exactly what, and got metal money back in circulation.

Our plane reached Tampico in the morning the day before the rodeo started; we did no fishing that day. We didn't even see the Panuco. The rodeo committee had banned all tarpon fishing in the river for a week before the big event, figuring that would increase the catch. So Felix and a couple of other Tampico men met us at the airport and took us to the hotel; then we went to his tackle store, and we saw the tackle we were going to use.

I wouldn't look at Hurt or Dave. It was the kind of tackle that opera-tors of a charter boat use, in self-defense, in taking landlubbers out to battle giant bluefin tuna. The rods were short and as thick as a billiard cue in the middle. The reels weighed three pounds. The line looked like a small rope. And at the end dangled a heavy ten-foot steel leader topped off by that mighty Pflueger Record spoon. I think it was listed as the No. 7 spoon, but I'm not sure.

"How come you don't use mullet?" I asked Felix.

"They hit the spoon much better," he said. "They seldom hit mullet at all."

This was cockeyed and I knew it, for the Pflueger Record is intended to simulate a mullet in action, trying to escape, and I knew that any time tarpon would hit the spoon, they would hit mullet. But . . . I was the guest. In the other man's fishing hole . . .

Dinner that night at the Tampico Club was one of those things you talk about years later. Tampico is famed for its rock crabs. We had them. It is famed for red snapper, caught over submerged coral reefs not far from shore. There can be no finer food than the baked snapper with salsa Veracruzana we had that night. And the papayas . . . and the aquacates, real ones, not what we know as avocado. This was Mexico, unadulterated except by early Spaniards. And the fact that Felix and one other man spoke English didn't bother me. I get along in Spanish, and Dave is completely bilingual.

Since I am conditioned to fishing practices of my fellow Texans, I was up long before dawn the next morning, "feeling" the air, speculating on prospects. A flat rule of mine in saltwater fishing, and other fishing as well, is that you greet the fish at dawn. I've seen hundreds of articles in print claiming that the theory is wrong. Should go by moon pull. I didn't bother to read them. I like to meet fish at dawn, but that day the meeting took place, after a number of leisurely discussions at the yacht basin on the river, at 9 o'clock. And it ended promptly at 1:00 P.M., after which fishermen gathered in the dining room of the yacht club for drinks and a leisurely dinner, then went home for a leisurely siesta. Ah, how charming the ways of Mexico. How sad that the "Nordic Horde," as I like to call gringo turistas, is forcing a change.

Then I saw our boats. Felix had chartered two. They were the river passenger-freight boats, about twenty-eight feet long, and with a canopy from bow to stern. Real nice for shade, which you learn to love in that tropical country. But we couldn't have done any casting even if we had brought our gear. I did ask Felix if he had any lighter tackle than the stuff he dug out for me. He and I fished from one boat, Dave and Hurt from the other.

"You're not used to the kind of tarpon we've got in this river," he said with pride. "The grandpapas and grandmamas stay here—the grandchildren go to Texas, where you catch them. You'll be glad you have this tackle."

The host speaketh . . .

So we trolled, if you could call it that, upstream until we reached the big bend where literally thousands of tarpon were showing—more tarpon than I had ever seen in any one spot before. And we trolled through them—and nothing happened. I couldn't figure trolling at that speed, about six miles an hour, maybe seven. On rare occasions when I do troll for tarpon, I barely move. So I asked Felix.

"The boat has only one speed," he said.

The host speaketh again . . .

I've encountered tarpon that would strike only at a lure racing along, but it was racing on the surface, and the conditions were different, as I will explain later. Sure, trolling fast often pays off if you're after sailfish. But the sail is a speed demon, a coldwater fish that likes to show speed. In general, tarpon, warm-water fish, are lazy . . . until they feel a hook.

On and on we trolled. Nothing happened.

Occasionally I saw some angler battling a tarpon. One fisherman, a fellow American, was pancaking a six-footer so hard when it jumped that it quit that nonsense in a hurry, whereupon the angler cranked it in. I also noticed that what little action I saw was taking place in the relatively straight stretches between the big bends, not in the bends where tarpon were concentrated.

In those straight stretches tarpon were on the move. I could tell by the way they showed when coming up for air—snout first, then dorsal fin straight up, then a tip of the tail. In the schools tarpon were rolling sideways, which indicated they were at least staying at or near the bottom, even though I had no idea whether they were feeding there, a question I sure cleared up later in a spectacular way.

I suggested to Felix that he have our skipper troll past one of those traveling tarpon and drag our spoons in front of the fish. Felix said the skipper knew plenty about tarpon fishing. In other words, it was time for me to quit telling him and the skipper how to catch tarpon.

I quit.

That morning Felix had two strikes—in fairly straight stretches of the river. Of course, there are no really straight stretches in any river untouched by man—there are no straight lines in nature, not even in the movement of light, as Einstein explained. There are straight rivers—or stretches of river. But they're manmade, and I'll tell you later about some fishing experiences in them.

I had only one lone strike—when the boat was coming about to head downstream. My big old lure was wobbling down toward the bottom at the time. There was so much slack in the line, I couldn't strike the fish. But later in the day we began mulling over the strike and decided there was something we might do the next day to get action.

So far as the rodeo people were concerned, the day was a glorious success. The 150 or so anglers, about a third of them from this country, brought in close to twenty tarpon, as I recall it, and topping the list was a giant almost seven feet long and weighing 197 pounds. In that rodeo any tarpon under five feet was considered a baby, so maybe quite a few smaller ones had been caught. They could not be entered. The smaller ones were there, however. And I regretted still more that I didn't have my casting gear, for I just knew I could have latched onto some of the four- and five-footers that I saw rolling, or traveling.[3]

During the four hours of fishing, I never saw one tarpon strike at the surface, except a couple that bounced into the air after hitting lures—not my lure. And I saw no mullet. This seemed real strange to me, for that broad, clear blue river certainly should be a fantastic feeding place for mullet. Maybe that's why it wasn't—that clear, blue water, with no place to hide. Mullet like shallow water, such as that on grassy flats in a bay, if it is clear, but where their enemies are, they like some kind of protection—murky water, a tide rip, a stretch of shallow shore. You don't find those conditions up the Panuco, and we didn't catch any tarpon. Dave and Hurt had two strikes and caught nothing. Fine fishing day.

# CHAPTER 4

# Noble Experiments

After that water haul on the first day of fishing, Dave and Hurt and I joined several other rodeo contestants at Felix Florencia's tackle store for the customary afternoon bull session. I cautioned my companions about saying anything that might wound the feelings of Felix or some other Tampico resident—I mean about criticizing their way of fishing. But we had to do something. We didn't want to spend three days hanging onto that mighty gear with the big spoon tugging at it. We discussed phoning home and having some of our gear shipped down on the plane next day. But . . . chances are the irreplaceable rods might be broken, and Felix, lending us his tackle graciously, would be offended. At the bull session all the talk was about the big ones that others had caught, and nobody was much interested in what we didn't catch.

I did notice several huge plugs for sale. The price was sky high, and after studying them, we were convinced that they would spin instead of wobbling when they were trolled at that six-mile clip. They would wind up the line—that's all.

I did arrange a shift in personnel in the boats. I told Felix I would like to fish from the other boat, with Dave, and let Hurt fish with him, giving the excuse that I would have a good chance of getting action photos when he hung a tarpon. Dave and Hurt and I had figured a bit of strategy based on the bump I had while the boat was making a turn. Dave, speaking Spanish the same as the Mexicans, could make the skipper do what we wanted. And he could use me, the famous writer, as reason for a change in

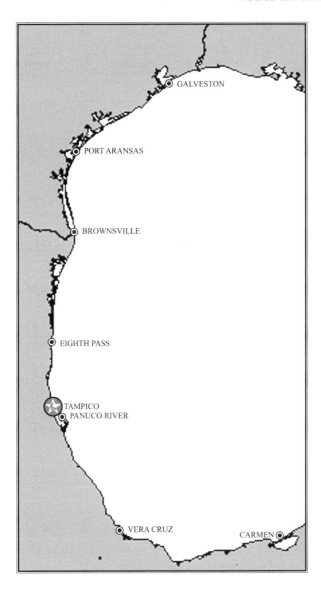

strategy. Hurt didn't mind but insisted that he shift back after we did a bit of training on our skipper. He'd be in the second boat the last day.

When we got to the tarpon, Dave asked the skipper to stop the boat momentarily. When it stopped, we let the lures go on down, then retrieved them—and Dave had a bump. But here came Felix in his boat, wanting to know if we were having boat trouble. So we trolled on, trying still another trick. We would bring the lure right up to the boat, then release tension and let it wobble down toward the bottom until it was a hundred yards away, then throw the drag back on. Nothing notable happened. And we had to give up after fifteen or twenty minutes because of the pull of that mighty Pflueger Record spoon.

I never could understand the aqua-dynamics of that spoon—don't know enough about physics. Since the outside—the bottom of the "spoon"—was down, you would figure that the chunk of metal would ride along the surface when dragged at six miles an hour. It would now and then, whereupon you cured the situation by letting out a bit of line. The spoon dug down. It swung horizontally through an arc of about four feet, and in the process it exerted so much pressure that tension of the brake would slip if you tried to reel the spoon in by simply cranking. So we had to pump our lures in to get them near the boat—raise the rod tip slowly, then reel rapidly while lowering it, and on and on. So our idea of hauling the spoon up to the boat and releasing tension, so that it would dig down, was abandoned after about twenty minutes. Too doggone much hard work.

"Let's try the damn straightaways and see if we can hang a traveler," I said to Dave.

He conveyed the message to Vicente, our skipper. Any time Dave is around, I let him do the talking in Spanish. We saw a few loners but never could get the boatman to put the lure where we wanted it. What he usually did was scare the hell out of the fish by practically cruising over it. So we cruised up to our cantina and took a break, consoling ourselves with the fine tequila. Back we came . . . and the same old story.

During the day other anglers caught enough big ones to make the day a howling success, rodeo-wise. Of course fifteen or twenty fish distributed among 150 anglers is not my idea of spectacular fishing, especially if I am among the 130 or more who catch nothing. But you string up twenty giant tarpon on a pole and you've got something to work with when it comes to taking photos—if your objective is to interest people here and there in the world in the rodeo. Felix did land a tarpon, one barely under the five-foot minimum for entry in the rodeo competition. And Hurt had a couple of strikes but did not make contact.

I made careful note that the most successful anglers were those who trolled what seemed to be a half mile back of the boat—it certainly was 200 yards or more. I'm accustomed to trolling, when I do at all, about forty or fifty yards behind a boat. One reason is that I usually have the kind of gear that won't stand up if a tarpon hits two hundred yards away—line too light and not enough of it left on the reel. But with that giant Panuco gear you could stop a six-footer dead in his tracks. So I decided the last day out I would troll way back, damn near the end of my line. I couldn't think of anything else that might be considered constructive. I had just about lost interest in the rodeo insofar as my own fishing was concerned. I began, on the third day out, haunting other boats, trying to get action shots—and since I was back with Felix, he didn't mind that suggestion.

I dedicated more attention, the previous night, to certain good things in life calculated to take my mind off defeat in the rodeo—mainly a nice cathouse not far from the center of town. I talked to Felix and he arranged for a friend of his, I'll call him Ricardo Villareal, to go with me to the favorite cathouse of businessmen in the city. In Mexico the attitude toward prostitution, which has always been legal, is quite different from the attitude here. It is pretty generally accepted that any man able to finance the procedure will visit whorehouses and maybe his favorite girl there—maybe eventually set her up in a little place of her own. There is no stigma attached, as there is—or was until the past few years—in this country. I'm not concerning myself here with relative moral values; I merely say that I have enjoyed this part of the Mexican culture down through the years—and with no feeling of guilt. I got Ricardo to go with me because I knew Hurt and Dave wouldn't. I didn't even ask them.[1]

You talk about getting my mind off the rodeo—I sure did. Beforehand I wondered a bit about my reception at the cathouse, since practically no other gringos ever went there. None in Tampico then. But I didn't have to worry, especially when I talked a little Spanish. The girls were lovely—that wonderful blend of Spanish and Mexican-Indian that has produced a race of people as fascinating as the Polynesians. As I say, I felt no sense of guilt. I grew up on the Rio Grande, and visiting cathouses in Mexico had been a part of my cultural pattern for a long, long time.

But I was terrified when Ricardo started driving the streets of Tampico. He drove without lights. At least without headlights. Only dim parking lights. And the street lights were equally dim—or missing entirely. I guess it was part of the wartime hysteria—blackouts on the coast. In Tampico, as in most other old Mexican cities, buildings run smack to the street intersections, so it's blind corner after blind corner. The idea in driving, as demonstrated to me by Ricardo, was to see who could honk loudest as he approached an intersection. The loudest horn won the right-of-way.

Ricardo must have had a special horn installed in his car. It was terrific—and he sure stopped cars at intersections, sometimes with only a few feet to spare. But we made it, and I switched from fishing, which is probably only a form of sublimation when practiced as a sport, to an entirely different kind of sport that doggone sure isn't sublimation of anything. And, for the moment, I forgot the rodeo. The next day it was back to fishing—hanging on again as that dopey spoon wobbled.

One pleasant difference between writing a book and writing articles for magazines is that in a book you can tell the truth when you get skunked—when you, the Great White Fisherman, spend three days fishing a river with thousands of tarpon in it and manage not to catch one. That's "negative" in the opinion of magazine editors. It was particularly embarrassing to me and Dave and Hurt, for all three of us had reputations in the world of tarpon fishing. Pictures of the two in action had appeared in many articles I wrote about tarpon fishing. And I can admit it here, although I went way around in circles to sort of fog the image of our defeat when I turned out the magazine article. The objective was to do justice to the Panuco. I did.

The third day I had a nice, sociable boat ride with Felix. I let my giant spoon out as far as I could—still no strikes. Felix had two solid strikes, and I was sure that he literally tore the hooks out the way he hit the fish. Dave and Hurt caught nothing, but there would be a return engagement. No river is going to whip down Dave and Hurt and me. We would have gone back in a few weeks except for something known as money, which I have mentioned before. Dave owns and operates a Spanish-language movie house in Brownsville, and he was just pulling out of the dread depression days.[2] Hurt was faced with closing his sporting goods store for the duration—you can't sell tackle and guns and ammunition if you can't get any. And me—I was to get $75, and no expense money, for the magazine article.

I told Felix we would be back the next year. "But we'd like to rent two skiffs," I told him.

"We wouldn't dream of letting you charter boats," he said. "We'll have the same two boats ready."

Oh yes? Over my dead body.

"Felix, I have a flat rule," I said. "The rodeo people can pay for the charter the first time out. The next time, we pay. And we want skiffs—small ones. We'll bring our own motors."

And so it was agreed.

# Mystery Tarpon

Dave and I felt a little uneasy as we slid the cartop boat into the Rio Grande and cranked the motor. It was wartime, and pilots of the Civil Air Patrol had a way of buzzing anything or anybody they spotted as they guarded our frontier. I never did find out what they were looking for. Nothing came across the river where we were except wetbacks and bootleggers bringing tequila. But it was buzz, buzz, buzz, as we knew from experience at the mouth of the river. The CAP men, most of them Hollywood expatriates out for a lark, were doing their thing.

We had a tough time getting permission to put boats in the Rio Grande, and we never did manage to get more than tacit understanding from U.S. and Mexico officials that they wouldn't bother us if we didn't cross the center line of the river, thereby invading Mexican territory. For reasons which I still do not understand, we had fished the mouth of the Rio Grande for eight years and not once did we go on up the river and take a look. We couldn't drive along the bank because there was no road. But we could drive to it at a number of places, on sort of cattle trails through the marsh and brush.

Now and then we had vague reports about some "big white fish" that Mexican *catan* fishermen hung. Catan is the Spanish word for gar, and commercial fishermen caught alligator gars in the river, dried the meat, and sold it. Dave loved the stinking stuff, just as he loved dried shrimp. I couldn't take the smell of either.

Sometimes the catan fishermen operated near the mouth of the river, where we could watch them. Usually they floated their baits, insides of a rabbit or a calf, out to the gars by using tiny rafts with miniature sails on

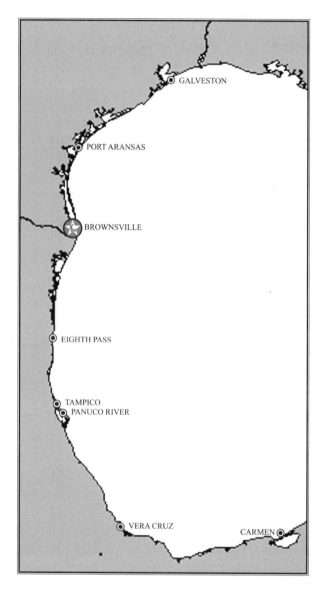

them. And on rare occasions a tarpon would take hold. Maybe he would straighten out the hook or bust the line. Maybe the fisherman would land him. If he did, he would dry the tarpon, salting it good, and hang it on the wall for future use. Most Mexicans living along rivers in that country like the flesh of tarpon. It isn't eaten in this country. I've tried eating a small one— pretty crummy and a lot of bones where bones have no business being.

Anyway, we had never bothered to drive across the salt flats and then through the brush to the few spots where the river could be reached between Brownsville and its mouth. It was waste country, populated mainly by feral donkeys that the late Snake King of Brownsville used to shoot to get meat for his lions until some smart cookie rounded the donkeys all up and drove them into Mexico, where there was a market for them. But after we got back from Tampico, we decided to do what we should have done eight years earlier—explore the river right there at home.

Now Dave and I, feeling a trifle like Columbus approaching land, rounded the big bend and saw something down in the next bend that we thought was a mighty school of mullet playing games.

They weren't mullet—they were tarpon.

It seemed that there were millions of them, although in retrospect I'll settle for a few thousand. We saw a lot more tarpon in the Panuco, but not so many crowded into such a small spot.

A hole dug out by the Rio Grande current as it rounds a bend may be two hundred feet across, seldom more. Such a hole in the Panuco may be almost a half mile across. So in the Rio Grande the fish jam up close together. And we knew the tarpon would gang up on our lures, so we leaned forward, trying to help the five-horse motor push the boat faster.

That's what we thought.

What actually happened was quite different—the tarpon calmly and insultingly ignored our lures. All the heroic things we figured on doing to those Panuco tarpon, once we got back there with our gear, might not happen. For a solid hour Dave and I cast, and the fish were so jammed up that one would occasionally throw water on us as he flipped his tail on the downslide. One actually touched the boat! A real insult if I ever had one. Time and again Dave and I would hit a tarpon as he rolled, just for the hell of it. We tried working the lure fast and working it slow. We tried going down eight or ten feet, then working the lure up. Dave even tried a trick we had used before, with fine results on several occasions—a trick I'll explain later in detail. He reversed the metal lip on the bottom of the plug's snout and brought the lure back riding the surface, fast. Nothing worked. We never even had a bump, and changing lures, from mullet type to shrimp type to spoons and back to mullet type, made no difference.

A big tarpon rolled about fifty feet away and Dave let go with a mighty cast, singing out, "Take that, you bastard." All Dave did was foul his line—a real mare's nest that took ten minutes to pick out. And all that time tarpon slapping the water and giving us the cold fish eye.

"I'm stuck on the damn bottom," Dave said, when he finally got the snarl out and started reeling in. "Now I'll lose a plug, and without even getting a strike . . . hey . . . hey, man! That's not the bottom. It's moving!"

I just sat there with my mouth open staring as a big tarpon came up from way down deep and burst into the air. He had plenty of slack, so he was able to fling the plug back, right at us, in anger it seemed. Then he slapped the water with his tail and went on back down to his "roost" on the bottom.

"What the hell . . ." I said, as I started reeling in my lure. I had let it sink to the bottom while I watched Dave's tarpon in action. Now, when I reeled in, I got resistance—and moving resistance.

"They're feeding on bottom," Dave said, casting out on the other side of the boat from my line and letting his lure sink.

Whatever took my lure turned loose—I was too surprised to sink the hook—so I reeled in and cast out, watching line flow from the reel as the lure sank—all the way to the bottom. When the line went slack, indicating the lure was on the bottom, I reeled in a bit, to take out the slack, then gently nudged the lure. Up the line came the message I'd been praying for—an answering nudge. I nudged harder, and the tarpon took hold. He seemed as deliberate about taking the lure as a man taking a bite of steak. I hit him as hard as I dared with that 20-pound test line. And stuck him. And at the same instant Dave began making those funny noises that some fishermen make when the stars shine.

A mystery was solved.

Both of us had a tarpon on. They were pretty rugged and going in opposite directions. Nobody could help anybody with the boat, something you need real badly when you tie into a six-footer with the casting gear we use. There was small call for worry. Both of us lost our fish. You lose plenty of tarpon when you cast plugs. Who cares? We never kill them anyway.

Dopey as it may seem, Dave and I sat talking for a bit, as though victory had been achieved and we could enjoy all the goodies of a glorious fishing session without hurrying.

"I should have listened to those catan fishermen," Dave said. "They've been telling me for years that tarpon in the river feed on some kind of great big river shrimp that stay on the bottom."

"Now I know why we caught nothing in the Panuco," I added.

"Did you see a mullet there?" Dave asked.

"Not one."

"They're feeding on the bottom on those shrimp or whatever they are," Dave said.

"Well, shall we tie into them?" I asked, as I switched from a mullet-type lure (one vaguely resembling a mullet in shape and action) to a heavier lure that is supposed to look like shrimp, at least to a fish.

"We'll murder the Panuco," Dave said, as he cast out.

It sure seemed crazy, sitting there, firing up a cigarette, waiting for a plug to settle on the bottom. Still—fishing with plugs. You figure it out, but we both had strikes. I lost mine on the first jump; Dave stuck his, a neat five-footer, and I maneuvered the boat as he whipped it down, eased it alongside, and took out the hook. We both took part in that operation, a very sound idea, as we knew from experience. We used only a short one-hand gaff, not the big pole that most tarpon fishermen use. And we were careful to gaff the tarpon only in the edge of its bony lower jaw, so we wouldn't injure it. You hold a tarpon's head out of the water alongside a dinky boat such as the one we were using, and you might be in trouble if he suddenly sets sail when pliers touch the inside of his mouth. So Dave got a good grip on the jaw with long pliers that we carried for the purpose, and I worked the hooks out with regular pliers, being careful not to hurt the fish.

No. 1 in the boat—or at it.

I'm sorry we kept no record of what happened that day. We had a strike, or at least a nudge, almost every cast. We hung half those that took hold solidly enough to get at least one jump. And we actually boated and released nine tarpon, ranging from a shade over three feet to one almost six feet.

The ratio of fish landed to tarpon hooked well enough to give forth a jump is extremely small, even when you've got a tight line at the time of the strike. It was much smaller that day because of the inevitable bow in the line from fishing on the bottom. Sure, you almost always get a bow in the line when a big sail or marlin takes off with the bait in its mouth. He may be three hundred yards away when he swallows the bait and you sink the hook when he makes his first jump, but the drag of three hundred yards of line is enough to sink a hook when you give it a boost with the rod. Just for fun, let out three hundred yards of line in a rough circle and try landing it with featherweight tackle. We had no such advantage. Tarpon were taking hold at the bottom, in about twenty-five feet of water. They weren't more than forty or fifty feet from us horizontally on most strikes. And they came straight up. Drag on that line bow did no good. So plenty of them kicked free.

Who cared? If you manage to get seventy tarpon in the air in one morning of fishing (we quit at noon), what more do you want? It was the wildest tarpon session I have ever experienced if you judge by the number of strikes and number of jumps—and the time span. Usually, your wild bursts of action are of short duration. We quit that day because of sheer weariness. Yes, I've heard and read thousands of times that old axiom that no real angler, no Great White Fisherman, ever quits while the fish are striking. I've done it thousands of times, especially when I was fishing for speckled trout (weakfish to you) or snook. So after five hours of battle we sat in the boat, meditating, surveying our sadly battered lures, sorrowing over two lost lures—and making threats against the Panuco. And I was thinking about the next morning, when Hurt and I would be out at the same spot. Dave was kind enough to claim that he couldn't get away from his business the next morning. We all knew that three men had no business casting for tarpon from that ten-foot, ninety-pound boat.

"I wonder what Hurt's going to say when we tell him," Dave said.

"He won't believe us," I said.

"Think we ought to catch one and take it in as proof?" Dave asked, and I could see the sparkle coming back into his eyes.

"No. He'll believe we caught tarpon if we tell him. What he won't believe is that he can't catch them the way we always do—that he'll have to still-fish on the bottom. Taking one in wouldn't prove a thing."

"I guess you're right," Dave said. "I'd sure like to be here and watch his face . . ."

"Okay, we can crowd in . . ."

"No. I'll let you tell me about it."

"Anyway, they may hit some other way tomorrow," I added.

"I'd bet on that," Dave said.

And, as things turned out, he would have lost . . . at least for a time.

# CHAPTER 6

# The True Believer

Eric Hoffer hadn't turned out that pile of pseudophilosophy at the time Hurt and I went back to the Rio Grande, in 1942, but I can say this for Hurt—he is the kind of man that will quit being a "true believer," Eric Hoffer style, and face reality even when it doesn't fit into all his preconceptions. And he doggone sure was no believer when Dave and I undertook, later in our day of glory, to convince him that the tarpon wouldn't touch anything except a lure on the bottom, maybe lying still. And sure enough, some did nudge lures that weren't even moving—sort of rooting them up. Those crazy river shrimp must be the slowest creatures in the sea.[1]

Since our whitewashing at the Panuco, Hurt had done what he realized was the inevitable—closed his sporting goods for the duration. But he moved most of what he had, especially his precious plugs, along with a dwindling supply of shotgun shells, into a little room in back of a print shop. He held forth there a major part of each day, and it remained a hangout for those of us who hunted and fished. So that's where Dave and I found him. A couple of other men were in the store. I didn't want them horning in on things until after Hurt and I made our trip, so I waited until they left.

One left in quite a huff. Hurt refused to sell him a couple of lures, even though the man was willing to pay double the price. "I sure won't come in here anymore," the man said. Hurt sort of smiled.

When he moved his dwindling stock into that little room, Hurt no longer sought business of people in general. What he did was nurse that stuff along and sell it, little by little, to those of us who had been his regular

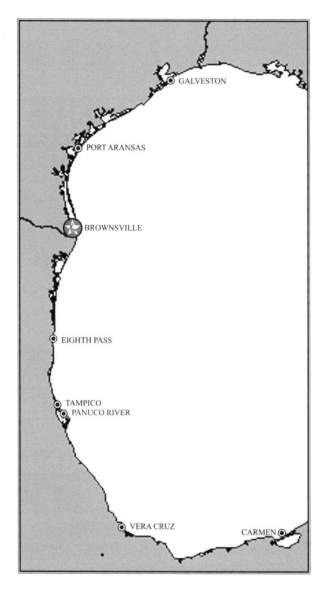

customers before war changed things. And by regular customer I mean people who wouldn't go to some chain store and buy a certain plug that was being sold at cut rate just to get customers in the store.

Hurt never sold anything at cut rate.

Now he still kept the same old prices, plus a tiny percentage increase because of overhead, on the gear he had, and he sold it to us at those prices. He wouldn't sell a plug for ten times the price to some customer who had bought stuff at cut rate. And he wouldn't let any of us—his regulars—overstock. He was particularly careful on .410 shotgun shells, which all of us used in hunting quail and white-winged doves—on rare occasions mourning doves. We hunted them only when white-wings were scarce. And we were careful. The limit on white-wings was twelve, and I would take only fifteen shells. It was the same with lures. If you choose a good leader, a plug for specks or reds will last almost indefinitely. It's not that way with tarpon lures, especially those with the crummy soft-metal hooks that we were getting.

So when the others were gone, we told Hurt. Dave and I were watching. Hurt was trying not to show any reaction, but his questions were a tipoff.

"You tried letting it go down pretty deep, then working it back up fast?"

"Sure," Dave said. "And slow and in between. You name it, we tried it."

"How long did you rest the plug on the bottom?"

"Maybe three or four minutes," I said, "plenty of time to fire up a smoke and meditate; we had to let him find it."

I was pouring it on a bit—so was Dave. And it was easy to see that Hurt was not a true believer—yet.

Finally, Hurt said, "What are we waiting on?"

"I'll pick you up at five in the morning," I said.

"I'll have breakfast ready."

On the run to the Tarpon Hole, as we decided to name it, I saw something I had not noticed the previous day—something that definitely worried me. I saw mullet. This could be bad—and it was bad I realized as we neared that spectacular gathering of tarpon. For now and then we could see a strike—a tarpon definitely lunging at, and probably catching, something at the surface. I would a hundred times rather hang a tarpon striking at the surface, when I can feel the jolt rattle my arms just as the plug hits the water. In contrast, still-fishing on the bottom is pretty dreary, until the tarpon surfaces. But for now I had visions of all that stuff Dave and I were explaining blowing into busted bubbles. Doggone slim chance of making a true believer out of Hurt.

In a river such as the Rio Grande, mullet move in shallow, slightly murky water, hugging shores or sandbars. It's protection against tarpon. But when mullet are moving upstream or downstream, and the silly things seem to be almost always on the move except on grass flats of a bay, they have to run the gauntlet at the bends. For suddenly the shallow shore isn't shallow anymore but changes to a bluff. So the mullet must cross to the other side of the river. And he has to race right smack over those hundreds of greedy tarpon. Numbers alone save him—or at least his species. For tarpon deal out deadly carnage at such times.

So as I cut the motor and let the little boat drift up to the tarpon (there was no breeze yet, so the anchor wasn't necessary), a tarpon blasted at the surface, Hurt put a plug on the spot—and BINGO! My theories were shot to hell in one blazing blast. I was so damn disgusted I just sat there for a spell, refusing to even watch the tarpon on his second jump, although I sure could hear him. Then I heard Hurt. "You going to help me or not?" he asked, and there was anxiety in his voice.

I quickly started the motor and took after his tarpon, a real hefty female that would need chasing. The chase wasn't very long. The tarpon straightened out one of those putty-like hooks and kept going, headed for the Gulf of Mexico for a rest until she got over the soremouth. But it was the same doggone thing when we got back to the tarpon. Cast—bingo. Cast—bingo. Who could complain?

I could. But I didn't say a word, and Hurt was gentleman enough not to gloat, not even flashing an "understanding" smile at me. Those infernal tarpon kept striking that way for more than a half hour, although we didn't spend all that time casting. We were battling fish.

I landed a four-footer, the size tarpon I would pick ideal for the kind of casting tackle I had. I boated him and eased out the hook in about ten minutes. Then Hurt got stuck to a five-footer, and it took longer to bring that one alongside. Even though we quit using the gaff, since just getting a grip on the tip of the lower jaw with the big pliers was quicker, it still took time to get the fish up to the boat and get the hooks out, and I knew Hurt was suffering. Sure, he loves to battle tarpon, but if plugs had been expendable, I felt sure he would have broken free, deliberately, after he got about all the jumps he was going to get—then hurried back to enjoy the blast at the surface again.

And do no moaning to me about the "cruelty" of letting a poor tarpon swim on off with a plug in its mouth. The tarpon gets rid of it. What he can't get rid of is something he has swallowed—a mullet impaled on a hook, for example.

All of a sudden things were quiet, except for the almost constant light noise—occasionally a big one—of a tarpon rolling while getting air. I studied the river carefully and saw that the mullet were gone.

Maybe all wasn't lost, after all. But I played it cool. I did just what Hurt was doing—continued casting my lure (mullet type) and working it the conventional way. Very near the top at times, by holding my rod tip high. Deeper now and then by letting it sink a bit and working it in slowly. I tried all the tricks. So did Hurt. Nothing, absolutely nothing. The expression on Hurt's face became grim. But he still wasn't a true believer, Mr. Hoffer.

At last I switched to the shrimp-type, heavier lure Dave and I had used the day before. We had found them better for this crazy fishing. I let the lure go to the bottom, rested it for a moment, then nudged it. Here came that sympathetic, understanding nudge being relayed to me up the line. I nudged again, being sure to take up slack before I did. That time I got a pretty solid rap, and I stuck him for keeps. When he surfaced and shimmied, the hook still held, and Hurt quickly put down his tackle and started for the stern of the boat.

"I can handle him," I said. "Go ahead and cast."

It was only a three-footer, so I had much more line, about two hundred yards, than I needed to handle him. Hurt cast out, all right. The same lure I had worked the same way. Converting the nonbelievers can be a rugged job, as devout church people well know.

I didn't tell Hurt how I hooked that tarpon. I didn't have to. He is one of the most alert persons I have ever known. He can see a quail behind him. So he knew. Yet there he was, casting the same lure, working it the same way.

I got the little fellow in and released him without any help from Hurt. You can hold a three-footer steady with big pliers. Then I cast out again, let the lure sink to the bottom, fired a smoke, then nudged. "I'm here, pal," came the message from below. I struck him—and when he busted the surface, Hurt put down his tackle, gave forth a heavy sigh, and said, "Okay, I'm a convert. Need any help?"

"Yes, I might . . . he's pretty . . . forget it."

He was gone.

I waited on Hurt—who had been waiting on me. I let him have the field, and he got just what I knew he would—a strike . . . by still-fishing on the bottom with a lure.

"You win," Hurt said. "Now chase him!"

I had to, for Hurt had managed to get latched to a six-footer. Children, mothers, grandparents, uncles, aunts, great-uncles—hell, they were all gathered in that hole. The clan. It's not always that way in the world of tarpon, fortunately. Many times you find small ones and nothing else. Seldom do you find only the giants, which is okay with me.

Chasing that tarpon began to present something of a problem, for he was heading straight for the Mexican side of the river. Even though the deep part of that hole may have been no more than two hundred feet across, the river was much wider there than along the moderately straight stretches. And on the Mexican side of the river was a member of what the Mexicans call Rurales—border guards. It is customary in Texas to refer to Rurales as counterparts of Texas Rangers. This may have been true in earlier days, when the primary function of the Rangers was to guard the state's frontiers against Indians and Mexicans. But the Rurales today are still pretty much border guards; the Texas Rangers are something entirely different—something that should have been phased out with the passing of the frontier.

Well, that Mexican river guard, with a big, bone-handle Peacemaker draped on one hip, just sat slantwise on his horse, coldly eyeing us as the infernal tarpon headed straight for him.

"Don't cross the center of the river . . . don't cross the center of the river . . . ," I thought.

What is the center of a river? If it's the center of the current, then the center line was way over close to the man on horseback.

Hurt had about two hundred yards of line, but you get a wrong impression if you think the line is effective right to the end. When you get down to twenty or so yards left on the reel spool, you can't judge the pressure you're putting on.

That river guard sure looked grim. So I sang out, as we hightailed it right behind the tarpon, "Tenemos permiso para pescar aqui." We have permission to fish here. The guard said nothing—just stared. Then the tarpon jumped and headed back right at us, and as I swung the dinky boat about and ran from the fish I heard the guard laugh at us being chased by a fish.

I couldn't go fast enough to outrun the fish. The five-horse motor, which actually delivered only a little more than three horsepower, wouldn't plane the boat with me and Hurt and our gear in it. The tarpon got all the slack he needed, and when he felt tension fade, he jumped and threw the plug. At the end of the day, Hurt hung and landed four tarpon, and I caught three.

"I still have trouble believing it," he said. "But you win. I'm not doing any arguing."

"Are we going to tell the great American public?" I asked.

"How about saying nothing for a couple of weeks until we can have the hole to ourselves for a few more trips," he said. "You can't always tell—those tarpon might get wise if they see enough lures."

I thought little of his remark at the time. I had plenty of chance later to meditate on the soundness of his prediction.

FDR (seated) shows off his catch, a fine tarpon taken off Port Aransas in 1937. Courtesy Dr. Fred'k McGregor Photo Collection, Corpus Christi Museum.

The author, Hart Stilwell, on the right, with a Soto La Marina snook caught in 1954. The fish would have been a line-class world record; however, Stilwell was using a treble hook, which invalidated record status. (Photo from *Austin American-Statesman*)

A Panuco "grandfather" giving a dazzling show of leaping ability. Notice the canopy on the Tampico riverboat used to keep shade on the Mexican sportsmen and their Anglo guests. (Photo from Stilwell's *Fishing in Mexico*)

A "nice-sounding" gill rattle from a Panuco tarpon. That giant cigar-shaped thing sticking out of her mouth isn't a Cuban; it's a Pflueger No. 7 Record spoon. (Photo from Stilwell's *Fishing in Mexico*)

The original Pflueger Record spoon in different sizes. (Photo from Wayne Ruby's *The Pflueger Heritage, Lures and Reels 1881–1952*)

This is an original No. 5. It's easy to see why they had to re-rig the tackle while trolling for the big fish of the Panuco. (Photo from Wayne Ruby's *The Pflueger Heritage, Lures and Reels 1881–1952*)

A well-used, tried-and-true Record Spoon. (Photo from Wayne Ruby's *The Pflueger Heritage, Lures and Reels 1881–1952*)

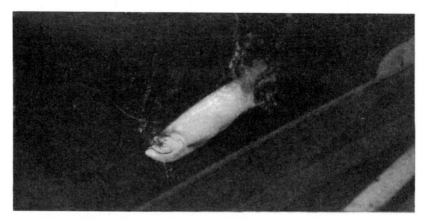

A silver king gives up the battle and comes alongside for a quick release. (Photo from Hart Stilwell's *Hunting and Fishing in Texas*)

*Field & Stream* Fishing Editor Ray Holland fighting an unseen fish at the famed Eighth Pass. This photo also appears in *Good Shot! A Book of Rod, Gun, and Camera*, by Raymond P. Holland with Bob and Dan Holland. (Photo Hart Stilwell)

Ray Holland with a fun-sized Eighth Pass silver king. (Photo Hart Stilwell)

Holland dragging a silver king beachside after a hard battle. Apparently, fish-handling etiquette was in its infancy. Dragging a fish removes the protective slime coat from their bodies, which can lead to infection and death. (Photo Hart Stilwell)

Holland with a beautiful Eighth Pass snook. (Photo Hart Stilwell)

A Vera Cruz silver king giving an aerial acrobatic show. (Photo Hart Stilwell)

Bink with a phenomenal Carmen robalo. (Photo Hart Stilwell)

"Doc" Dean rolling a nice snook up on a Carmen beach. (Photo Hart Stilwell)

"Doc" reaching into the "mangles" to wrestle out a wayward fish. (Photo Hart Stilwell)

A local "Indian" displaying a Carmen dinner. (Photo Hart Stilwell)

The pesky pargo that seemed to be everywhere in Carmen. (Photo Hart Stilwell)

Hurt and Dave wading the Soto La Marina for trout, reds, and snook. (Photo Hart Stilwell)

Hurt displaying a great stringer of speckled trout. (Photo Hart Stilwell)

An impressive display of Texas's lower Laguna Madre speckled trout and red fish. (Photo Hart Stilwell)

Getting up close and personal. Wading with leaping tarpon. (Photo Hart Stilwell)

A nice stringer of Port
Isabel speckled trout.
(Photo Hart Stilwell)

Shallow water, leaping tarpon from the newly dredged Brownsville Ship
Channel. (Photo Hart Stilwell)

They laughed when we sat down at the piano. They didn't laugh when we began playing tunes on a fishing line. No kidding, you can play tunes on a fishing line if it's tight enough. I fished for several years with a screwball trumpet player who loved to thump out little tunes on the line. He tightened or eased off tension to get different notes, and sometimes he got sore as hell if the fish disturbed his tune by making a run. The guy was nuts, but he was a lot of fun while he lasted.

The other contestants in the second annual Tampico Tarpon Rodeo watched carefully as we got into two little skiffs and latched on our three-horse motors. They examined our tackle and were puzzled—like the guide at Topolobampo, on Mexico's west coast, who tried to hoist a 12-pound snook into the boat with my 10-pound test line. He was puzzled. He wanted to know why I used such a line. The regulars, both gringo and Mexican, shook their heads in disbelief as they fingered the 20-pound test lines and looked at the dinky (to them) reels with no brakes and the long, fragile, whippy rods.

And this time we had plugs—the right kind. It's true they were a bit battered. And as a precaution against further destruction by the big ones in the Panuco, we had wired the two sets of treble hooks together and then attached the wire to the eye on top (or in front) of the plug. At least we wouldn't lose any hooks unless the line broke. And we had dug out a few remaining Swedish steel hooks that we had left and put them on our plugs for the occasion. For some odd reason, all the other contestants in the

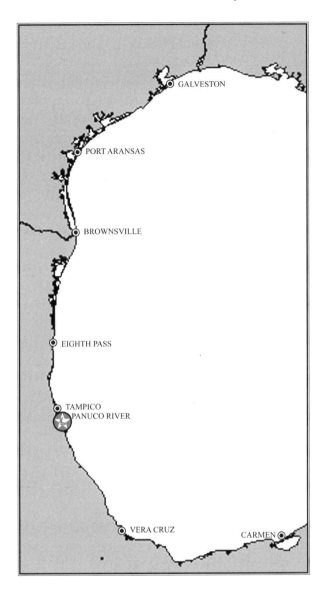

rodeo seemed to think it wouldn't be quite proper to do anything but drag that Pflueger spoon for three days. So away they cruised, and we buzzed slowly along, one boat heading upstream, one downstream.

There were four of us—Dave Young, Hurt Batsell, a Braniff Airways pilot named Bill Longino, and I. Bill fished with Hurt, Dave with me. Dave is not competitive, and I quickly adjust to his attitude. If we are wading shallow water near a bay shore, tossing out "floating spoons" for speckled trout, we don't bother to count the catch. Hurt is competitive, and I adjust to his attitude. I don't like myself when I'm competitive.

Dave and I headed upstream—maybe because we remembered the shady little cantina with the fine tequila. The four of us didn't fish the same spot because we figured that too much commotion might scare some of the fish. And there would be no foul-up of lines, something that can easily happen when boats are close together and tarpon are quite active.

As we approached the tarpon in the bend, we could see that they were merely rolling—no blasting of mullet at the surface. We figured working at or near the surface would be merely a waste of time, so when I cut the motor and we drifted in range, both of us cast out the heavy (seven-eighths ounce) shrimp-type plugs and let them go to the bottom. We cast into the wind, what little there was. That made it easier to keep a tight line as the boat drifted slowly through the tarpon. And casting the other way, we would have drifted over our plugs, which may or may not be such a hot idea, something I'll discuss later.

Both of us started to light cigarettes—the tarpon didn't give us time. Evidently, the slight movement of the boat gave the plugs just the right amount of nudge, and here came the message up the line. From that moment on, it was happy day. And I was sure in a mood to gloat, something I seldom do. That time the memory of the whitewash on our first trip came sharply to mind, reinforced by a few comments I had heard about the three "Great White Fishermen" from north of the Rio Grande being skunked. We couldn't keep a plug on the bottom a full minute without feeling a nudge—then a strike. These tarpon took hold quicker than those in the Rio Grande.

You can see an airborne tarpon almost a mile away, and soon we began attracting an audience. The Mexican anglers were more curious than the gringo, most of whom at least knew about casting plugs for tarpon. Also, the Mexicans were more polite.

Maybe Dave would be doing battle with a fish, and I'd be handling the boat. One of those river launches would stop some distance away, the fishermen careful not to foul our line. Then when Dave boated—or lost—the tarpon, the fishermen would ease on up and start asking questions. I let Dave do the talking when the questioning was in Spanish.

Those Mexican fishermen were positive that we were using carnada—live or once live bait. Even when we showed them our plugs, they were skeptical, for they had watched us (evidently with the aid of binoculars) and asked how we could make fish strike a piece of wood lying still on the bottom.

"I'll show you," Dave said—not in a bragging way at all, for he isn't that type, but just with confidence that events justified. So he cast out, let the lure sink, said a few words to our Mexican visitors, then nudged the plug. Up he came! I gloried in the way the fishermen talked at such times—and I sure was happy I could understand what they were saying.

Gloat, Stilwell! It's your turn. I did.

The fireworks were continuous. But we were losing more fish on the first jump than we did in Tarpon Hole, mainly because they were bigger. The tarpon were mangling those shrimp-type lures, made of wood. Later, fine plastic plugs of the same type came out. But we'd get a plug back with hooks jerked loose, dangling from the leader wire we had used to fasten things together. I think the wood was cedar. First, the tarpon would bust off the heavy varnish or lacquer or whatever kind of paint was on the plug. Then they'd split the plugs. I finally switched to an old reliable, a mullet-type plug that was old but durable—and had good hooks. And I managed to boat one.

"He's over five feet," Dave said, as he held the fish alongside after removing the hooks. "Want to keep him and haul him in?"

"Hell, no," I said. "I don't want to win any prizes. I just want to show somebody that we can catch a fish."

By that time, 1943, I had decided that I would never compete in another fishing rodeo, at least not one in Texas. I had seen so much crummy lack of sportsmanship put on display by "sportsmen" that I didn't want to even be in a rodeo again. That one in the Panuco would be my last. And it was quite different from the typical Texas rodeo—and different from the fishing roundups of today in Texas. For in our fishing contests a lot of valuable prizes are awarded. And if you want to see the sportsman at his worst, watch him as he competes for a $5,000 boat or some other such prize. In the Tampico rodeo the awards were cups—that's all. And they went to the biggest tarpon, not the greatest number or the most pounds.

I knew the odds were all against our bringing in any tarpon big enough to win a prize. The way to land a monster is to sink the mighty hook of a Pflueger Record spoon all the way through the bone of his jaw and work him over with heavy tackle. We didn't have that kind of gear, and we didn't want it. We were fishing for fun and enjoying it more and more as word passed along the river, from boat to boat, and the curious began assembling in larger numbers to see the "crazy Americans who are catching tarpon with plugs on the bottom."

Those curious soon began really bugging us, especially my fellow Americans. They figured that if we could catch tarpon in that school, then they could. So they began trolling through the school, then circling it, coming closer and closer to us. At times they threatened to cut our lines, which they could not see until a tarpon jumped. We motioned for them to move away. They ignored us. They had a right to get into the middle of the action. Sure they did. But after thirty minutes of catching nothing—and listening to our tarpon rattling gills—they would reluctantly cruise on off. And here would come more fishermen. They were like Hurt when we took off for Tarpon Hole. They were not true believers. Give them three days and see.[1]

Several times Dave and I quit fishing because of the clutter of boats, and one of those times we made the run on up to the cantina for a tequila and a bit of rest. The bartender, Benito, told us proudly that he now knew about American money and he would be glad to take any that we had. We didn't have any—and no one-peso bills torn in half either. The Mexican government had stopped that. Then back to the school of tarpon for another session.

That day Dave and I kept a record. I wanted to know. We had a total of a hundred and twenty-seven bumps at the bottom, had sixty-three tarpon hooked well enough to get at least one jump, and actually boated eight. Dave caught one that I'm sure was over five feet, and I urged him to take it in and enter it.

"They need them for pictures for the turistas," I said.

"Let somebody else lug dead tarpon in," Dave said. He doesn't think any more of rodeos than I do—he had fished with me in two or three rodeos in Texas before our Tampico trip.

So we eased up to the dock shortly after one o'clock with nothing to enter. Yet the anglers were gathered, or gathering, there to talk to us—maybe to buy some of our "magic" baits. And you might bear in mind that there are situations in which people there at the fishing hole really consider a lure as a bit of magic. Dave and Hurt and I ran into that situation on a trip years ago at the mouth of the Soto la Marina River, which is north of Tampico. When we began hauling in fine redfish by casting spoons, the native fishermen gathered around us and began muttering, and Dave said,

"They're getting upset. They think these spoons are magic and that we're going to take away all their fish. We'd better do something."

"Tell them they can have the fish," Hurt said. That eased their worries.

And so they wanted to buy our lures—I was offered twenty dollars American for one plug, the plug I had on my line when we tied up at the dock. We told the anglers, most of them Mexicans, that the plugs would not stand the pressure applied with their heavy tackle.

"Then how about buying that whole outfit," a Mexican angler said to me, pointing to a spare rig in the boat. We always take spare rigs in such fishing if we are a long way from home. The man offered me three hundred dollars for the rig.

"I can't sell it to you," I said. "I can't get any more because they're not being made. The war."

They didn't believe us and I sensed the hostility. We had something special that we were hoarding so we could show up everybody else.

"And spoons are best for the big tarpon," I added.

Sure, we would have spread some lures around as a gesture of international goodwill if we could have replaced them. The only others available were locked in Hurt's little semiprivate tackle shop.

After a leisurely early afternoon lunch and a siesta, we joined the bullfest at Felix's tackle store, and the first thing I noticed was a completely bare wall where there had been, the previous year, a big display of monster plugs. They were made of wood, then had an oddball gadget attached to the lower part of the snout, a piece of metal bent so that it would make the plug wobble. And they were loaded with gang hooks. The things were originally made for muskies, I was told. And when we examined them the previous year, we knew they wouldn't work if trolled from those launches because they would simply spin at that speed. We knew. We had tried them in the Rio Grande—just reeling in fast. But all were gone.

"They had bought them all out even before I got back here," Felix said. "They're going to show you fellows up."

"They've already done that," I said. "I counted twenty-one tarpon on display out there. We didn't bring any in."

Bill and Hurt, fishing downstream, had about the same luck we did. Continuous action, but nothing really big. A couple of five-footers, four smaller ones.

I didn't make any comment about the lures spinning, even when Felix tapped the top of a package containing six of those plugs.

"I phoned from the clubhouse and had these put aside for myself."

The plugs wouldn't even sink—had to fasten a sinker on. And they were worthless for casting unless you had sturdier gear than we did, for they weighed around two and a half ounces each compared to our seven-eighths-ounce plugs. When most of the other people were gone, I said, "Felix, would you like to fish with us? I've got a spare casting rig, and you can use any of my plugs you want to."

"Thanks," he said, "but I'll work them over with these plugs."

"They won't troll at that speed, Felix," I said.

"Why not?"

"They'll spin—just wind up your line."

I wasn't getting through to him. You seldom do when a fisherman gets that gleam in his eye—a fisherman gazing upon fine beautiful plugs, big enough for the he-man tarpon, the machos. Felix reminded me of an old Mexican ballad that goes, "I love to sing into the wind because it brings my songs back to me." I was singing into the wind, and my words were coming back.

We had company at our new tarpon hole the next day—and I say new because Dave and I went downstream that morning, while Bill and Hurt went upstream. I spent more time watching other anglers, those with the big plugs, than I did fishing. We were right—the plugs twisted lines up until getting the kinks out was an irritating job. The angler had to let the line back out in the water with no lure on it. Then here came Felix and his fishing companion—my "pal" Ricardo from the cathouse ventures. The boatman cut the motor and the launch eased up fairly close. I waited.

"Won't work," Felix admitted. "Spins, the way you said."

"Want one of my plugs?" I asked. My shrimp-type plugs would not spin, even at a fast clip.

"No thanks," he said. " I know you need them."

"I think you can make that plug work, Felix, if you don't mind a suggestion."

"Fire away," he said.

"Put a sinker on it, cruise upwind past the tarpon, then stop the motor and drift back through them, let the plug go to the bottom, and just nudge it if it isn't moving."

He tried it, promptly hung a tarpon, and just as promptly reeled in a plug all crushed with the hooks straightened out. Those hooks wouldn't take the pressure of that heavy tackle unless the angler eased way off on tension, and doggone few anglers do that unless they're old hands at the game. Felix tried it again—and reeled in another mangled plug. He gave up.

Then an idea came to me. It was almost impossible to do any casting from the river launch in which Felix and Ricardo were fishing. But there sure was something else that might be done. When the day's fishing was over at 1:00 P.M., after about the same kind of continuous action as on the first day, I talked to my companions about the idea I had in mind for the last day of fishing. "Those guys have been real fine to us . . . ," I started.

"I'd say Ricardo has been unusually nice to you," Dave cut in, thinking of the cathouse visits.

"Anyway, suppose I get in with them and have them tow one of our boats along; then they can get in it, one at a time, and really get some action."

I was absolutely certain that Felix and Ricardo would not spend the whole day in that open skiff in the burning sun. The Mexican sportsman demands his comfort.

"I'll let them use my rigs," I said.

"They can have my spare," said Hurt, and Dave volunteered too.

"Can you three fish from one skiff?" I asked.

They said they could. The skiffs were heavy and had a broad beam compared to the little cartop boat we used in river fishing for tarpon. My companions also loaned me a few of their precious plugs. Felix and Ricardo were charmed at the idea, so charmed that they decided to cruise a bit farther up the Panuco and find a "new" tarpon hole where they would be alone. As we neared the school, I noticed two things: First, the percentage of small tarpon, even as little as two feet, was greater, even though grandma and grandpa did show now and then; second, this meant that they were feeding on mullet.

"I don't think we'll have to fish on the bottom," I told my companions as we rigged our gear. I selected three mullet-type plugs, which are much better when tarpon are hitting at the surface.

"What's the difference between this hole and the others?" Felix asked.

"I saw a tarpon hit a mullet. Let's try it near the top."

We did, and the tarpon banged into those plugs. Hard!

Before we started fishing, I handed each of my companions a couple of the knitted thumb stalls that we use in tarpon fishing. There was no internal drag in our reels. I noticed both Ricardo and Felix put the thumb stalls away in pockets. They dug them out and put them on in a hurry after the first strike. That sizzling line will burn a hole in your thumb if you press too hard. In a way I guess it was fortunate they didn't put the thumb stalls on at first, for they clamped down so hard the line might have busted. They sure let go in a hurry. I had told Felix and Ricardo in advance that they had small chance of landing a truly big one with our gear.

"Let the others win the cups," Felix said. "Man, all I want is some action—the kind you fellows have had."

Tarpon struck at the surface for about an hour, during which time the three of us, fishing from the skiff with an outboard motor latched onto the stern panel, brought five tarpon to gaff. One, caught by Felix, was over five feet, so he decided to keep it and add to the total catch for the rodeo. Then the mullet moved on—going upstream—and we began still-fishing on the bottom with plugs.

"Sure feels silly," Ricardo said.

"Who cares if—hey, something's nudging my plug," Felix said. Ricardo and I reeled in quickly, and Felix hung and boated another tarpon, but it didn't go quite five feet.

What delighted me was hanging into and landing a couple of fish only a shade over three feet. I decided that on my next trip to the Panuco I would really explore. You find smaller fish way up some rivers, and I wanted them. Then came grandpa nosing around—and Ricardo stuck him solid with the real fine Swedish hooks on that old plug of mine.

Felix and I reeled in, and I got the motor going in a hurry. It had plenty of power, so I could maneuver the boat as Ricardo did a truly beautiful job of handling the fish. He had learned so much battling jumpers from fishing for sails off Mexico's west coast. He whipped that one down. And as near as we could figure, measuring with my rod, which was seven feet long, the big silver king would go about six feet, four inches. A trophy tarpon, maybe. And it did win a trophy, although not the top one. I can't remember the exact system they used in that rodeo to determine the prize fish, probably because I never brought in a fish and was embarrassed about asking. But I think they added the length, in inches, to half the weight, in pounds. Anyway, a fat lady tarpon won top prize for the day—but Ricardo lugged off the cup for third prize.

That night Ricardo and Felix and my companions and I gathered for our farewell dinner at the wonderful Tampico Club restaurant—and that's all it is, a restaurant. We had a little going-away gift for Felix. I told my companions I was going to give Felix four of my precious plugs, so each of them pitched in two more plugs. We proudly spread them out on the table in front of Felix, but he immediately covered them with a napkin.

"Man, those rodeo fishermen would murder me to get these. Don't ever say a word."

He gave two of the plugs to Ricardo.

"We just couldn't do anything about rods and reels and lines to go with them, Felix," I started.

"Do no worrying. I know a place in Mexico City where I can get what I need—from a pilot for Compania Mexicana."

Compania Mexicana de Aviacion is a Mexican airline, originally part of Pan American and still a subsidiary. Some of the pilots, who flew to seaports often, picked up tackle of various kinds now and then.

I felt real good about the way things worked out. Felix had been the perfect host. And, of course, Ricardo had been my companero in certain delightful extracurricular activities. You can feel that way about your hosts if you don't deadhead—if you're under no obligation from the beginning. So you feel bighearted when you release your grip on some "killer plugs" that are in short supply. And so, Panuco, hail and farewell. Thou didst meet thy equals. And memories of the shameful water haul the previous year no longer caused pain.

# CHAPTER 8

# Bay of the Iguanas

The only disappointment about our trip to Carmen was the Southern Cross. I had never seen it before, and I more or less expected something spectacular. That dim "little" constellation wasn't a third as interesting as the iguanas.

Carmen is "around the bend" of the Gulf of Mexico, a short distance east of the southernmost tip. The Mexicans call the waters there Bahía de Campeche—Bay of Campeche. Americans call it the Gulf of Campeche. The coastline at Carmen runs east and west, and I never adjusted to that, not even on later trips. I'm too firmly conditioned to the coastline running north and south, as it does along the Texas coast and the northern coast of Mexico.

Tarpon and other fish at Carmen had seen practically no artificial lures. Only resident of the town who used lures was an expatriate Englishman named Cecil Bronson who had settled there many years before and started an import–export business.[1] For a long time, while the British Empire flourished, British sportsmen followed the flag, and you could go to a remote spot and find an Englishman with the inevitable fly rod. If there were no trout, he would plant some. In fact, Britishers did that in some of the mountain streams in Mexico. Now, of course, you can't escape your fellow American, no matter where you go.

It was difficult concentrating on tarpon during my first visit to Carmen because huge snook and barracuda kept attracting my attention—busting my lures. And there were dozens of fish of other kinds worthy of attention, since the big bay there, called Laguna de Términos, is a fantastic fish

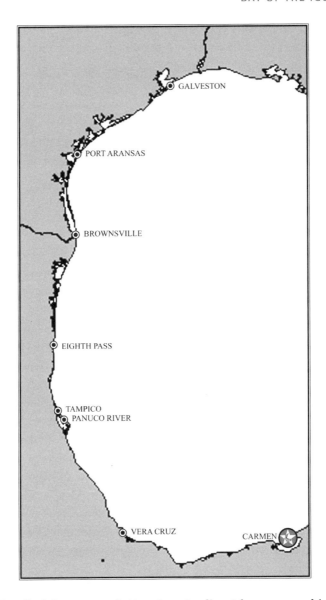

GALVESTON

PORT ARANSAS

BROWNSVILLE

EIGHTH PASS

TAMPICO
PANUCO RIVER

VERA CRUZ

CARMEN

trap. It is called the Laguna de Terminos (endings) because two big rivers and half a dozen smaller ones empty into it, bringing a bountiful supply of plankton and other food for small fish out of the tropical jungles of the Isthmus of Tehuantepec. The main rivers are the Candelaria and the Grijalva. Unfortunately, we never did manage to go up them. They were far from our base of operations, and our oddball boat couldn't go faster— or slower—than five miles an hour. But the Englishman said there were plenty of tarpon in the rivers, including babies on up them a distance, and also snook even farther upstream. And plenty of pargo around the mangroves lining the streams near the bay.

There was more, much more—countless millions of fine white shrimp, which my fellow Americans would soon be catching by the hundreds of tons. And there were speckled trout, Bronson said, although I never saw any. I did see what I went there to see—thousands and thousands of tarpon. And I caught what I wanted to catch—tarpon and snook and big barracuda and pargo (a kind of snapper) and other game.

Snook look and act much the same as tarpon. They are lean and long and silvery, but are easily distinguishable from tarpon because of a black line along each side, from gill flap to tail. They even have the typical underslung lower jaw of the tarpon. And they come boiling in the air just as a tarpon does, once they feel the hook. Real battlers. Snook get as big as seventy or eighty pounds, although I've never caught any much larger than thirty, which is plenty of gamefish—and plenty of fine eating fish. That's one big difference between the two: Snook are first-rate food fish. And this fact is contributing to lean days for the fish.[2]

There is a close similarity in the range and feeding habits of the two fish. Both go up rivers—snook a bit farther than tarpon. In fact, there is a fish, perhaps just a breed, of snook in Mexico called the river snook. It is heavier and darker colored on top. It goes back to saltwater only to spawn, spending the rest of its life in rivers. The coastal fish, in contrast, is leaner and lighter on the back. We call him a tide-runner.

Carmen is at the western end of an island, and we made the thirty-mile trip to the eastern end of the island in an ancient Ford, weaving through a jungle of coconut palms. Then we crossed the two-mile-wide inlet and settled in a fishing village called Aguada. The name comes from the Spanish aqua, meaning water. A tiny trickle of fresh water runs into the big bay near the village.

We slept on air mattresses on a cement floor in a home at the village. Bronson had made arrangements for the room and food. He knew my companions on the trip, Dr. Roy B. Dean and Bink Goodrich, both of Mexico City. I was living in Mexico City then, gathering material for a book on fishing in Mexico, published the following year, 1948.[3] Bink and Doc said I should go to Carmen, so we went. And the memory lingers on, for Carmen at that time was untouched by gringo hands except those of Bink and Doc, American expatriates; and Bronson, English expatriate.

Only souvenir from the activities there a few years earlier of some American military people, particularly engineers, was the paved strip at the airfield—and that cement floor in the home at Aguada.

Some officer had set up a fishing headquarters there. So you couldn't say it was virgin fishing, which wasn't any particular shock to me since I've run into that kind of fishing hundreds of times in my wanderings around Mexico before the Nordic Horde started south. And I mean freshwater fishing as well as saltwater. I had been the first gringo to fish way up in some little mountain lake where huge rainbows fought for the right to get hooked.

It took us five hours to cross the two-mile inlet. No, we didn't have motor trouble; we had fish trouble. Every time somebody let a lure over the side of our dopey boat, a fish took it. A tarpon, a snook, a barracuda, a thirty-pound pargo. So it was stop the boat and man the guns.

Chato, our guide, saved a twenty-pound barracuda for eating purposes. He wrapped it in a wet sack and put it in the shade. We could eat what the Mexicans call bacalao, and they're referring to the dish, not the kind of fish in it. The Spanish call codfish bacalao—in Mexico the dish is called that, and it doggone sure isn't codfish, for they don't move into Mexican waters.[4]

Doc and Bink, who knew the layout, had Chato move just inside the submerged reef that extended across most of the mouth of the inlet. That's where we started raising big barracuda and pargo—by casting, not trolling. The barracuda is another jumper—the kind of fish I love. And for plenty of reasons, one of which was demonstrated that day. The jumpers hightail it for open water and fight like a man. Fish that don't jump dig for obstacles—and so the pargo were cutting our lines on shell and dead coral in the reef.

During my later years of fishing, I practically abandoned fish that would not jump—all except the speckled trout and his much larger cousins, the totuava and corvina of Mexico's west coast. Although the speckled trout in general seldom jump, a big one is almost certain to come to the surface and make a sort of popping sound as he shows his snout momentarily and jerks back down. And they don't burrow into the barnacle-encrusted growth, such as mangrove, that line many waters along Mexico's coastlines.[5]

Since we were using tarpon tackle, we were able to handle some fairly large pargos in spite of their efforts to dig in. I noted the big difference between this snapper and the red snapper that is so popular among Texas fishermen. The Carmen snapper is built more like a redfish and is a pretty good battler once you keep him clear of obstacles. The red snapper—well, I've caught a few and you can have them. You must use a mighty weight to get a shrimp, or even a lure, down to them (shark will take it if it doesn't go down fast), then you haul up that chunk of lead and a dead fish. Depressurized too fast.

Doc said we had to get on across the inlet and eat before the mosquitoes moved out of hiding and started feeding. So, reluctantly, we headed straight for the village. That sure was a funny boat, a twenty-four-foot double-ender with a one-lung motor that must have been imported from England by Bronson's father. Chato had to spin a big flywheel with his hands to start it. Then his helper, a little boy named Manuel, stood pouring some liquid from a can into the motor. It was oil, not gas. The motor had no reverse—and only one speed, about five miles an hour.

At our quarters, a home owned by a widow, Dona Isabel, we relaxed with the aid of a local drink called cana, which is also the Spanish word for cane, or sugarcane. The stuff was fiery, but Bink and Chato knew what to do. Chato got some coconuts and with one deft, backhanded stroke with a machete, he cut a neat little opening, along with a lid, at the pointed end of the coconut.

"Takes skill to cut just far enough so a man can turn the flap back, yet leave a hinge for it," Bink said. "A beginner would whack it off. You need the flap to keep out insects."

Well, he poured some cana in the three coconuts and the stuff tasted fine that way. And we put away a huge amount of bacalao that Dona Isabela cooked for us, then got inside mosquito nets suspended over air mattresses on the floor and went to sleep to the music of two thousand disappointed mosquitoes.

Bink and Doc are late risers. They're conditioned to that kind of life in Mexico City, where you finish dinner late, get to bed around one o'clock in the morning, maybe get up at nine, and take a siesta in the afternoon. Although I'm a siesta man, I have never been able to cure the habit of waking with the dawn. A hangover from my days of working on an afternoon newspaper.

So at dawn the next morning I went outside, got my tackle, and set off to have a look at the shoreline between our home base and the point where bay and gulf waters met. That's usually one of the liveliest spots if the tide is right, and I consider a fast incoming tide best. I dropped the lure in the tide rip. No action. After fifteen minutes of fruitless casting, I remembered an experience at the once famed Eighth Pass on the northeast Gulf Coast of Mexico.

The Eighth was a snook assembly spot for quite a few years, but on one trip we could get action only one way—by casting out into the tide, nudging the lure back gently, and letting it sink in the tide rip. I'll tell you later about that Eighth Pass trip, which I arranged when Dan Holland, fishing editor of *Field & Stream* at the time, thought I was stretching it a bit in what I had been writing about the spot. So at Carmen I tried the same trick, casting into the edge of the current, then letting the lure sort of spin as it settled in the tide rip. It never got all the way to the bottom—a lean, lantern-jawed snook took it, and pretty soon bombs were bursting in air.

Snook are easier to stick than tarpon because of the almost translucent thin membrane that stretches between the two bony sides of the lower jaw. But a hook is likely to pull out of that membrane. Best bet is to stick it in the jawbone, something you don't always do.

I slid my twenty-pounder onto the sand, far enough so he wouldn't flop back, and at that moment I saw a small tarpon roll. I flipped the plug near the spot, let it sink only a couple of inches, and tapped it. More bombs bursting in air. Maybe I should have felt patriotic. What I actually felt as I lost the small tarpon, then hung a snook, was that any gentleman in my place would hotfoot it back and get Bink and Doc to come join the fun. I've never claimed to be a gentleman, but I did, after landing my second snook, head back to home base, dragging the snook along for eating purposes. Finest eating fish are those broiled just after they're killed, and I wanted broiled snook steak for breakfast.

On my way I had almost a hand-to-wing battle with a lot of buzzards blocking my path as they gorged on a big dead fish. You get away from what we usually refer to as the American Way of Life, and you might be surprised to find that people in many parts of the world seldom kill wild creatures just for the hell of it. Nobody bothered those buzzards, so they thought they owned the beach. I had to threaten them with my fishing rod to get through.

In about fifteen minutes Bink and Doc and I were glorying in what I call selective fishing—that is, a situation in which you can pretty much take your choice between two equally great gamefish by the way you work the lure. That has happened to me quite a few times, and later I'll tell you about one wild experience in "selective fishing" for redfish and speckled trout.

That morning if we wanted a tarpon, all we had to do was write "tarpon" on the lure, drop it where one showed, let it sink two or three feet and rap it. For snook we had to be careful not to move the lure, lest a tarpon grab it, as the thing wobbled on down close to the bottom.

Doc was using spinning gear, which was relatively new then. It had just come to Mexico City from France, and he had only about eighty yards of line on that reel that looked so offensive (upside down and backass) that I wouldn't touch it for a long time. So he was being careful as possible to get down among the snook, most of which he could handle, especially since they took off up the bay and parallel to shore, jumping as they moved. Of course Doc marked "snook" on his lure.

Unfortunately, tarpon can't read signs, and pretty soon Doc got himself all tied up with a flashy five-footer. You don't stand flat-footed on shore and stop a tarpon that size with eighty yards of light line on your reel—not even if the line is much heavier than what Doc was using. So Doc uttered a few paternosters (or a fisherman's equivalent thereof) as the tarpon sailed away. Maybe the paternosters were genuine—at least the line broke at the lure, and soon all three of us were back in action, Doc and Bink fighting snook while I roughed up a three-foot tarpon. Even though I have been in many situations where I could pick between two fine gamefish just by the manner of handling my lure, such joys have not come often when tarpon and snook made up the combination.

So I'm going to take a break now from my Carmen story and go back to an earlier one. There is plenty of time to tell more about Carmen and the Laguna de Terminos, and since that area is still one of the best—the least damaged by man—I should tell more. Some of the other spots—they're barely memories. Those trips I made to them when they were at the peak of glory take on more importance—to me, not others. Let's switch to a great bay that I saw "created"—and not by man. And that I saw "ruined"—mainly by man.

# CHAPTER 9

# New Bay—Crazy Fish

All fishermen know what happens when man builds a big new lake. Fishing is wild. And all fishermen soon learn what happens when the man-made lake grows old, at ten to twenty years: Fishing goes to hell. But few people have ever explored a huge, brand new bay that was created (I probably should say opened up) by nature, not man. I am among those lucky few.

Along the flat coastline of southern Texas, there is a bay more than a hundred miles long, ranging from five to fifteen miles wide. It is called the Laguna Madre—Mother Bay. Almost exactly the same kind of bay, also called Laguna Madre, extends for about a hundred miles south of the Rio Grande on the northeast coast of Mexico. For many years prior to 1933, the Laguna Madre of Mexico was listed as a dead bay, although it really was not dead. There was no inlet from the Gulf of Mexico; at least not enough drain off into the bay to force a cut through the long strip of sand that walled it off from the Gulf. There was, of course, life in the big bay prior to 1933. But not the kind that would interest a fisherman.

Then in 1933 a mighty hurricane literally brought the Gulf inland for many miles, cutting a dozen or more inlets through the strip of sand. And here came the fish—millions of them.

I had just started fiddling around with fishing at that time and paid little attention to occasional reports about the wild fishing in the Laguna Madre of Mexico that was building up after the hurricane. Furthermore, getting down to that bay, which starts about twenty miles south of the Rio Grande, was a tough deal. Bear in mind that we were in the middle of the

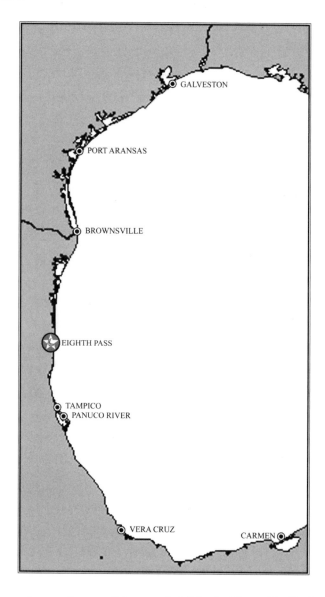

Big Depression, and none of the people I fished with could afford a puddle jumper to fly down south and land on the beach near one of those passes, as we in Texas call inlets. Getting there by car or truck was really a job— salt flats with no roads, passes that could not be passed. And, according to the reports we began getting, the best fishing was at the Fifth Pass. The First and Third were fair—the Second and Fourth closed soon after they were opened.

The reports we got came mainly from commercial fish operators— enterprising Americans who were moving seining boats to the northern part of the bay and using trucks equipped with huge airplane tires to bring the catch back. Tremendous catches of big speckled trout and redfish and snook. Obviously, those fish moved into the bay, probably from the south. They doggone sure weren't there before the hurricane, and they couldn't have reached such size in a year or two. It is amazing the way saltwater fish will find and swarm into a new feeding area.

Several of us finally made it all the way down to the Fifth Pass because of an adventuresome soul in Brownsville named Vincent Stevenson. He rigged a marsh buggy of sorts, equipping it with pontoons. He used an old Model T Ford truck and got power to cross the First and Third Passes by latching a big propeller onto the stern and rigging it so that the rear wheels of the truck would turn it. Real dopey—and once we barely escaped being washed out into the breakers in the Gulf.

And so we made it to the Fifth Pass.

It was crazy. That's the place where I first enjoyed the luxury of selective fishing. By that time—I think it was 1936, when FDR caught his tarpon— we had switched to lures, and they were ideal in the Fifth, which was so narrow that we could almost cross it. But we soon became annoyed by the redfish, which you may know as channel bass. If you think a man is out of his mind being annoyed by redfish that strike too actively, you are failing to consider the other fish there in the pass—speckled trout. They were huge specks, averaging around five pounds, compared to what we were accustomed to catching in Texas waters—a little more than two pounds average. But redfish kept horning in and taking the lures. Some were husky brutes, twenty pounds or more. Sure, catching a red that size is a lot of fun. Thousands of times I've prayed they would strike. But the specks, even though a bit smaller, were a lot livelier—our kind of fish. So we found that if we worked floaters and kept them moving at a fast clip, we could avoid the redfish and catch only specks—just a red now and then.

We didn't realize it at the time, but one reason for the wild feeding of those fish was an approaching hurricane. Man must have all sorts of gadgets to know when a hurricane is approaching—fish and other creatures just know. Those fish were gorging in anticipation of a long period of lying on the bottom in protected water, doing no feeding, as the hurricane swept over.

It wasn't a big hurricane. But it was big enough to cut a channel through the narrow strip of sand behind us, so there we sat, the truck settled down to its bed in the sand, water from crashing waves creeping on across the point of land and into our camp. Another slight rise in the tide and we would get the full impact of the mighty waves—and would be swept on out into the big bay.

The hurricane experience soured me on the Laguna Madre of Mexico for a year, but Vince kept dropping around with stories about the Eighth Pass, which he said was ten times more spectacular than the Fifth. So finally a group of us made the trip with him. I paid little attention to it at the time, but on the trip to the Fifth I saw no tarpon. At the Eighth . . .

We were the first gringos to camp on the south side of the huge inlet. There we met tarpon . . . and snook . . . and specks that topped ten pounds . . . and reds that topped forty. And when I wrote a story about the trip and sent it to *Field & Stream*, I got a wire from Dan Holland, at that time fishing editor of the magazine. "If there is a fishing hole like that in the world, it is the duty of the fishing editor to try it," he wired.

"Come on down," I wired back.

He came.

Actually, the Seventh Pass, which was in the process of closing, and the Eighth Pass were one, for at high tide water comes over the lump of sand between them. So in the dinky boats we had, it was necessary to swing far out in the bay to get away from rollers that were sweeping in from the Gulf.

It was almost dark when we settled down in camp on the south side of the Eighth, and we hit the sack early, for the trip was long and tough. But way along in the night a noise—one that I had learned to love—awakened me. Fish were feeding at the surface right at the inside edge of the pass, not more than a hundred feet from our tents. I lay trying to figure out what fish were feeding. There was the plop, like a plunker doing its job, of a speck. Then a slash which I figured must be a snook. Then a blast which I knew was a tarpon. You learn to read those sounds just as a trapper learns to read what some animal "writes" on the ground.

I sat up and lit a smoke. Pretty soon somebody else did the same. It was Dave Young.

"You hear what I'm hearing," I asked, as softly as I could, for all eight of us were crowded into one big army tent.

"I hear," Dave said. "And to hear is to obey."

"What's going on," somebody else asked. It was Dan Holland, the city dude from New York.

"Fish are feeding," I said. "Let's go."

I don't like to fish at night. I doubt if I've fished at night more than a dozen times in my life, even though it seems to be extraordinarily effective in taking certain fish—crappie while fishing under a light, for example. Other fish also feed well at night. Years ago when I was writing regularly for Esquire, Arnold Gingrich, the editor, wrote me asking for help in catching seven big bass in a pond near his home. I'm no authority on fishing of any kind, but if you sell fishing stories, you'd better be ready to come up with a suggestion in such situations. I did. I told Gingrich to go out and catch his bass at night. I was astounded when he wrote saying that he had triumphed. But he didn't convert me—that noise of feeding fish did, at least for the moment. I just couldn't endure that noise. So I flung a floater out in the middle of the feeding fish, figuring that any other lure might get stuck on the bottom if I had a backlash, something you've got to figure on when you fish at night and can't see the flight of your lure.

I got that noble plop of a fine speck and whipped him down—about a seven-pounder, which I released, since all the fish we kept on that trip was enough to eat. And Dan Holland hung a snook, which we could identify when moonlight showed that black stripe along the side. Fine going— Dan landed the snook, a fifteen-pounder. Dave hung a small tarpon but lost it.

Everything still okay. As I recall it, we had just changed to nylon lines then—I think we made the trip in 1938, but I could be a year off. You would be amazed if you should try that first nylon line made for fishing. The stuff stretched about an inch to the foot, which meant that when you got a strike thirty yards away, sinking the hook was impossible—about like using a rubber line. Also, the nylon would wear quickly from casting, and unless you broke off a few feet after fifteen or twenty minutes of casting, you were likely to see your plug sail on off into eternity with no line to slow it. But—it was better and less expensive than silk, which wore out in a hurry in saltwater. And linen line won't work through a level wind.

So for a time it was cast and bang. Then a fight—or a fish lost on a jump. Then I hung a tarpon. He wasn't a big one, but any tarpon except a baby presented problems on the light tackle I was using—at night. I tried to follow the course of the fish on runs, but it was hopeless—he'd leap off to one side and I wouldn't even know it was my fish, especially since very little message was relayed to me along that rubbery line. Finally, he kicked free.

We made so much noise that soon all eight of those in the party were gathered along the water's edge fishing. Things got out of hand then. One angler would cast over another's line—a fish would run over or under two or three lines. Somebody would have a backlash and start shouting when a fish struck the lure and finally busted the line. Pretty crazy fish—real crazy fishermen.

I finally got a king-size backlash, and I didn't even bother to work on it. I just hauled the line in by hand and put my gear aside. Spectacular or not spectacular, this wasn't my kind of fishing. I wanted to see what was happening. So I stood and listened, to fish feeding on shrimp (big school moving in), to fish striking, to fishermen shouting. Soon I noticed that Dave and Hurt, the old regulars, had also quit fishing and were standing watching. The others fished on—until the shrimp worked their way through the pass and on up the bay, and all action came to a halt.

"It's even crazier than you said it was," Dan remarked, as we went back to the tent, passed the tequila jug around for a nerve settler, then crawled back onto our cots.

We came to a dividing of paths at dawn that morning. The great schools of specks had moved into the bay, following the shrimp. In such situations shrimp hightail it (backward if being pursued) out to what we call the grass flats—shallow water, grassy bottom. Hurt is a dedicated speckled trout fisherman, and if he can raise them on a "floating spoon" out in the flats, he'll abandon tarpon to others. So he and three more of the group headed up the bay in pursuit of specks.

Dave and I are far more dedicated to tarpon, so we decided to try the pass. Dan Holland fished with us. For a half hour nothing of note happened except that a group of "outside agitators" came swarming in on us. To an arch conservative, anybody from out of time who has slightly different views is branded an outside agitator. To a fisherman glorying in complete isolation, anybody showing up on the scene is an outside agitator. And here came six or seven people, town dudes, judging by their tackle and the way they cast. Backlashes—and more backlashes. That's what they were getting, trying to cast with rods too short and stubby and with reels too big and line too heavy.

Dan and Dave and I were disgusted, since we felt crowded at our "own" casting spot. Crowded can mean strangely different things. A rat isn't crowded by ten people to the apartment; an eagle is crowded if he can see a human being. So we started to take off and follow Hurt and his companions. But at that moment one of the dudes started shouting. He had picked out a backlash, and when he started cranking in, a snook took his lure. Then another dude got excited—and then Dan and Dave and I elbowed our way back into the thick of things.

Bear in mind that the year was 1938, long before Dave and I learned about those bottom-feeding tarpon in the Rio Grande and long before Bink and Doc and I figured out how to take snook at Carmen by going down. We started casting out into the edge of the current and letting the lures go down—all the way to the bottom if nothing hit. We just nudged the lure a bit at intervals as it went down. And all of a sudden we were battling snook. These were big snook, ranging from twelve pounds to more than our little scales would handle—twenty-five pounds. We estimated some at thirty-five.

I think Hurt saw the flashes of light—and even though he was several hundred yards away, he could tell they were battling snook, not tarpon. So he began working his way back toward us, taking a speck now and then, but not raising them as he had hoped to. Unfortunately for him, a big school of tarpon moved in just before he reached us, so the first thing he did was hang a five-footer on light casting gear, and away went a lure and a small chunk of line.

But he solved the tarpon problem. He did just what Bink and Doc and I did at Carmen ten years later: He let the lure weave on down through the tarpon, if that was agreeable to them, then rap it when it got down deep. Soon he had what he wanted, a fifteen-pound snook slashing at the surface. The snook seldom comes straight up, after the manner of tarpon. Most of the time the snook lunges along more of a horizontal line, the way he does in feeding at the surface.

Well, Dan and Dave and I and a couple of others preferred tarpon, and we had casting tackle a bit heavier than Hurt was using, so we could hope to handle anything up to five feet. At one time that morning five of us had tarpon on at the same time. When I lost mine, I reluctantly put my rod down and got out the camera. I wanted to get a shot of three or four tarpon leaping at the same time. Of course I never did, although several of the shots showed five fishermen battling game. I wanted proof for Dan to take back with him, and he got plenty of it.

And we had our fishing spot to ourselves. The dudes, who were really pretty nice guys, even if they did invade my territory, all headed for the nearby surf. Vince told them they could catch twenty- and thirty-pound redfish there, and that's what they wanted, and that's what they got.

We were completely exhausted when the fish finally moved on—even too tired to eat until we had a couple of solid tequilas to lift the spirits.

Fishing was the same day after day. By the time we left the Eighth, our hands were covered with cuts from handling snook and tarpon and other fish. And the saltwater sort of corroded the cuts. It did worse on our legs. I left there with saltwater sores, as they are called, that a doctor couldn't cure for two months—I've still got scars on my legs from that trip.

That trip had a real funny windup.

The last morning, when we were to cross the pass—actually two passes—early and head for home, fish started that popping, slashing, lunging business in the pass near our tent. I raised up on an elbow, fired a smoke, and listened for a moment.

"So you hear it too," Dave whispered.

"Yes, but I'm not going to do a damn thing about it."

I went back to sleep to the sound of feeding fish. We estimated that we had caught more than three thousand speckled trout, along with several hundred redfish and at least three hundred snook. The trout were monster. We never caught a small one—the kind that Texans catch now, ranging from a foot to maybe a foot and a half. We caught fish from four pounds up to eleven, by actual weight. The snook averaged fifteen pounds. And first prize in the speckled trout division of the 1971 Port Isabel Fishing Roundup (Originally the Port Isabel Tarpon Rodeo) went to a fish that weighed two and a half pounds. At the Eighth in 1938 you could have used him as bait.[1]

Even though we planned an early takeoff and promised each other there would be no fishing, somebody threw a plug out in the pass and hooked another snook. And, of course, soon we were all busy catching snook and we kept putting off and putting off the time of departure. We kept none of the fish—only those we had already eaten. The truck on the north side of the Eighth would get us back to an eating place by noon—we thought.

Well, when we finally stumbled—from sheer weariness—up to the truck, we found that it wouldn't run. Vince was waiting for a part that had to be brought from his base camp, on the north side of the First Pass (where we had expected to eat). There was no food on our truck. We had stayed two days longer than expected, and everything was gone. We had returned probably fifteen thousand pounds of edible fish to the water—now we didn't have even one to eat.

"Somebody has to go catch a few fish," Vince said.

But who? We were weary, nursing our saltwater sores, sunburned, and the idea of catching a fish to eat the thing appealed to none of us. So we drew straws to see who would have to go out a little way in the bay in a boat and catch a few specks.

Dan and I lost.

When I cut the motor and we got ready to cast, he said, "Do me a favor and never say a word about this."

"About what," I asked.

"About drawing straws to see who would have to go catch a fish. Dad would have a really good laugh on me."

Dan's father, Ray Holland, was editor of Field & Stream at that time. Later Dan entered the Navy in World War II and suffered a back injury from some kind of explosion on ship. But he recovered and returned to writing in the outdoor field. And when he and his father and a younger bother whose name I don't recall brought out a book, mainly reproductions of photos, some of the shots I made of Dan at the Eighth were included. [2]

That was the Eighth before man worked it over with nets and seines. I'll tell you more about it later—how it is today. Real sad.

# CHAPTER 10

# The Lamps of Mexico

Oddball little gadgets sometimes serve to link two momentous events separated by quite a time span—in this case more than fifteen years. At Carmen the gadget was a lampwick.

Dr. Roy B. Dean, one of my companions on that first journey to Carmen back in 1947, was at that time a practicing orthodontist in Mexico City. He retired ten years later. Doc could do things with metal—part of his professional skill. So after his first trip to Carmen, one that he and Bink made only a short time before the three of us went there, Doc noted some things that did not please him. The best all-round lure seemed to be a feather jig—or simply a feather, as fishermen call it. I think the first feather lures were made in Japan. At least we referred to them as "those Japanese lures." Barracuda quickly chewed the feathers off Doc's lures. Neither tarpon nor snook have teeth, although tarpon will eventually wear out a feather. Barracuda do the job in a hurry.

So when we took off, Doc was all stocked up with a new kind of "feather." He made some lures fastening lampwicks to a small chunk of lead in which a hook was embedded. There were plenty of kerosene lamps in Mexico then, hence plenty of lampwicks. I guess there are still plenty of lampwicks in Mexico. I'm not sure you can buy one in this country except in some novelty store.

Doc did a neat job turning out those lampwick lures, although they sure looked gooney to me, and I wondered about the drab, off-white color. The color was quite a contrast to the bright colors on the Japanese lures. But, even though fish are not color blind, most of the gaudy color on lures is

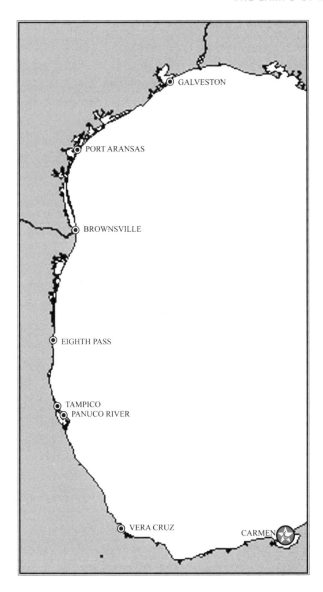

put there to attract fishermen, not fish. We clearly proved this in the early days of our speckled trout fishing by simply fastening hooks and a screw-eye to an old-style wood clothes pin and catching bushels of fish. No color on those lures. But at times color—probably intensity rather than the color itself—can make a difference. I won't go into that now, for I'm busy with Doc's lampwick lures.

Later experience, at Carmen and elsewhere, leads me to believe that

Doc had more action on that trip than we did because of the extra weight of his lampwicks, not necessarily shape or color or action. His lures were so heavy I had to cast with a big sweeping motion, so I didn't use them at first. But the snook kept saying, "We want lampwicks," and Doc gave them what they wanted. And finally Bink and I yielded and borrowed lures from Doc.

The lures would settle quickly to the spot, near the bottom, where snook were gathered—so we gathered snook. Then we decided that we should try to explore some of the big bay. Doc and Bink insisted I had an obligation to do so since I was going to tell the great American fishing public about this brand new hotspot.

Well, our exploring sure fizzled in a hurry, partly because of that oddball boat, partly because of the size of the bay—thirty miles by fifteen miles. Two fairly large, but not very long, rivers, the Candelaria and the Grijalva, empty into the bay, and there are many smaller streams coming out of the jungle. You get a wide variety of game at the mouth of any of these streams. It would take an angler three months of steady travel and fishing to really explore the Laguna de Terminos and streams emptying into it. Our time was limited to five days—our speed to five miles an hour.

We finally got to the mouth of one small stream—I don't recall its name—and had a lively time with small tarpon for about an hour, after which the tarpon moved and we began hanging pargo. As I have mentioned, the pargo—a snapper—found there is shaped pretty much like a redfish and fights about the same way, being quite different from the red snapper caught over submerged reefs in the Gulf of Mexico. The Carmen pargo is a better gamefish, and we got a kick out of making them strike our "floating spoons," three-eighths-ounce spoons that we could keep on top by holding the rod tip high and retrieving fast. But with that kind of light gear you give up on pargo pretty soon if they are around mangroves, for they dig in—and when the line touches a barnacle, it's gone. And there are always barnacles on mangroves—mangles, the Mexicans call them. Also oysters on some of them. It was the same old story: The fish I love, the jumpers, head for open water and fight like a man; the nonjumpers burrow into obstacles.

We never tried the surf, although Bronson, the Englishman, said it was working with big gamefish. I believed him; I'm just not a surf fisherman. I don't like being banged around by waves. On the last day we decided that I also owed my gentle reading public in the United States some information about really big tarpon, and we figured a scheme to help us catch one.

Since Chato's ship would cruise at only one speed—five miles an hour—we solved the problem of achieving proper trolling speed by rigging a sail on the boat and trolling smack into the breeze. We would troll through the channel, then make a fast run back and troll again. We used those huge Pflueger Record spoons Felix used in the Panuco. The idea was to hang a big one solidly and land him.

Doc quickly got fast to a giant, well over six feet and weighing, we estimated, at least 180 pounds. He battled it with his sailfish gear, standard light tackle for billfish, at least at that time. And Doc knew how to handle that gear—at various times over a period of years he held records in fishing for sails with light tackle. After we brought that one to gaff, Bink and I trolled on until each of us landed a tarpon around the six-foot mark.

That night we ate baked iguana and drank cana from coconuts and speculated on whether the three of us would ever again sit out in the open at that spot and look at the Southern Cross. We never did. But—the objective at that time was achieved.

Then came that funny lampwick lure coincidence more than fifteen years later. Hal Hassey, a man who owned and operated a printing plant in New York, somehow got a copy of my book, Fishing in Mexico, and read about that trip to Carmen. He suddenly decided he had been spending his life the wrong way, so he sold out and went to Carmen and opened a first-rate fishing lodge. He was going to make a pot of money on gringo anglers, and he wrote me asking if I would be his guest on a trip to his lodge—and, of course, write a magazine story. I said sure, if I could get an assignment and if he would just give me and my companions whatever reduction he wished on the tab. I don't make long fishing trips alone—and, as I have mentioned, deadheading doesn't always work out right.

So I wrote Zack Taylor, at that time associate editor of Sports Afield. And here's another coincidence—I got from Zack almost the same message I got from Dan Holland way back in 1938: If there is such a fishing hole, the associate editor ought to visit it. I told him to come on—I was sure of my fishing spot, just as I was of the once famed Eighth. Want to guess what greeted us when we pulled up to shore in front of Hal Hassey's fishing lodge?

Lampwick lures. And being used by Mexican commercial fishermen.

They were standing on the beach, at almost the same spot where Bink and Doc and I stood back in 1947, and they were hurling out big lampwick lures on handlines. And they were catching snook. And as we docked, one of the fishermen hung a five-foot tarpon, so we had the pleasure of seeing a genuine battle. That fisherman, using no gloves to protect his leather-tough hands, whipped the tarpon down and hauled it in. And kept it. Tarpon are eaten by people along the east coast of Mexico. But the lampwicks charmed me. Exactly the same as those Doc had "invented," although the lead was heavier.

It wasn't the first time I've seen that sort of thing in Mexico. On one of my first trips to Tampico my companions and I made a short run south in the Tamiahua Lagoon to fish for speckled trout and snook. We had fine action, and the Mexican guides made careful note of the lures we were using—small, fast-sinking plugs that had a faint resemblance to shrimp, at least in the area of action. Quite a few years later some friends and I went back to that lagoon—and ran into a "school of fishermen," all using plugs made in the exact imitation of the ones we used. Theirs were carved from the horns of cattle.

One wrinkled old man, fishing alone, really had a system going. He was paddling his little dugout-type craft (it was made of planking) and had the heavy line tied to the big toe of his left foot. The toe was about twice the size of his other big toe. I guess there is a streak of meanness in every human being—at least in me. I sat there watching him, hoping that a stud jackfish would grab the lure and really give that toe a battle. Maybe plenty of jackfish had already done that, judging by the size of the toe. The old man was catching fish—and on our lures. And the commercial fishermen at Carmen were catching snook—on Doc's lampwick lures. And at our fishing spots.

Out of the past shall come lampwicks—like oil for the lamps of China.

To Zack that was a miracle fishing hole. We found that we could catch snook way out in the wide pass—by going deep for them. And Hal Hassey, the Yankee bookbinder, made me look a bit sad one morning because he had the kind of feather that would go down much faster than mine. His was so heavy I couldn't cast it, so I had none along. I finally borrowed one and sort of flung it out slantwise and caught snook. And we caught tarpon and Zack was a true believer. And we caught big barracuda and big pargo.

I didn't say anything about it to Zack, but I noticed a great difference in the fishing in 1962 compared to that first fishing trip back in 1947.[1] The reason I said nothing: that old deadhead handicap. We were getting our trip at cost. It's a bad idea—and that was my last. But I could easily see the change—caused almost entirely by my fellow Americans, who were in the process of catching practically all those great white shrimp out of that wonderful bay.

The shrimping started soon after my first 1947 trip—maybe because of what I wrote about the bay. Soon American fish houses, headquartered at Brownsville, Texas, were flying those monster, premium white shrimp out of Carmen by the thousand of tons.

Shrimp attract gamefish. Take away the shrimp . . .

I spent much of my time on that trip noting the difference in the fishing in that fifteen-year span. There were about a tenth as many tarpon and about a tenth as many snook, judging by the time and effort necessary to get action. Sure, Zack thought it was wonderful. And I agree that any man who demands better fishing than we had in 1962 is a hog. You can't compare any well-fished bay with a virgin bay and fail to note the difference. Part of that difference is, of course, caused by anglers. A hundred anglers fishing in one area might catch twenty tarpon. Four anglers might catch almost the same. And we had company on that trip—several other parties of gringos trolling and casting. But the big difference, in my opinion, was the vanishing shrimp.

You kill a bay by polluting the water or taking out the shrimp or taking the gamefish out with seines. Anglers can't do the job—although they can change the nature of the fishing through a process of education. Yes, you can educate tarpon—and snook. Evidently there has been still more change in Carmen since my last trip. For Hassey left it and moved on, around the huge lump of land called the Yucatan Peninsula, setting up in a "brand new" fishing spot along the coast where Mexico and Guatemala meet. But . . . that spot will eventually be crowded too.

I tried to locate Chato on that trip but had no luck. He had either died or moved, and getting details was difficult since Chato is a popular nickname in Mexico. What I wanted to do, especially after watching those commercial fishermen handlining for snook with the Dr. Roy B. Dean Special, was give Chato some of my plugs that were sure-fire poison on pargo. I tried them and verified it. The plugs got ten times more pargo action than feathers. I finally gave the plugs to Jacinto, skipper of our fishing boat, and he was delighted. I didn't have to tell him how to work them, for he had watched the gringos fish—including us.

But one thing I forgot to tell him—don't put one of those plugs anywhere near a tarpon. It would strip the hooks off a plug fastened to a heavy handline. So as we were boarding our taxi for the trip back to Carmen, I took a long last look at the inlet—and saw Jacinto do a lovely job of flinging one of those plugs way out. Then I saw a six-foot tarpon latch on. The line went sizzling through Jacinto's work-hardened hands until the tarpon reached the end, then the silver king sailed on, carrying with him a few hooks jerked from the plug.

That was, as I said, my last journey to "Iguana Hotspot," as some of my friends called it. And I sometimes mull over the possible changes during the ten-year interval since that trip. I wonder about the iguana, now that he is on the popularity list of "pets" in this country. I meditate on these "cultural accidents," as Herskowitz might have termed them, and form a mental picture that might even intrigue Charles Addams.[2] I see a tarpon, a six-foot silver king, in a fish bowl in some suburban home. Maybe he will survive there. But I don't want to get deeply involved right now in that business of survival, even though I do think it is possible the tarpon may be placed on the list of endangered species.

I want to get back to fishing.

# CHAPTER 11

# The Little Children at Play

Then there was the day when we met the babies—tarpon ranging from eight to fourteen inches. The introduction took place at a small arroyo extending inland from the Laguna de Tamiahua, a bay that starts at Tampico and extends south about sixty miles along the coast. It would be nice to say that we learned something that day about where baby tarpon come from. We really didn't. And nobody else seems to be certain—the ichthyologists and marine biologists are in agreement on one point about where baby tarpon come from. The storks have nothing to do with it. From there on everything is confusion, as I will explain later in relating my frustrations in attempts to find out about the life cycle of tarpon.

I had never seen tarpon that size before, even though I had been fishing for the silver king for twenty years when my companions and I spotted them in the little arroyo. But there they were in that little ditch. Of course I had read about anglers catching baby tarpon on fly rods in the Florida Everglades and in some little rivers of Cuba. But I kept hands off that area, and for a very good reason. Several writers for the outdoor magazines had stories now and then about tarpon fishing in Florida and the West Indies, and they sometimes mentioned the babies, the fly rod size. Those writers never invaded "my" territory—Texas and Mexico. So I was careful not to horn in on their territory—Florida and the West Indies.

As my companions and I stood on the bank of the arroyo watching the show, I had a definite feeling that we were watching children play grown-up, trying to imitate mama and papa. There was something funny about a ten-inch tarpon surfacing or maybe blasting some tiny fish or crustacean.

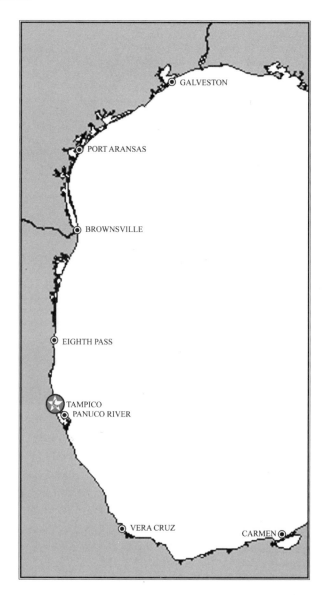

It didn't seem exactly real to me. But I wasted little time on that line of reflection. I hurried to my tackle box and dug out the tiniest lures I had—quarter-ounce spoons. Then quickly rigged my lightest tackle—featherweight rod, undersized four-ounce reel and ten-pound test line.[1]

My companions were doing the same. We were getting ready to "do battle" with the children. And as we skipped the tiny lures along the surface, it was bang! bang! bang! Those were mean children. Killers.

As so often happens when you pursue a gamefish throughout a big chunk of its range, our meeting with those babies was purely accidental. The original objective of our trip to Tampico was to do more "research" in that big Tamiahua Lagoon. Then we were going to return to Tampico and work over the tarpon in our favorite river, the Panuco, before returning to the States.

I had fished the northern part of the bay before, accompanied by two longtime fishing companions from Houston, Felix Stagno and Bill Saylor. We caught some mighty speckled trout and a few snook but saw no tarpon. On that trip the native Indian commercial handline fishermen, who supplied the Tampico market, were astounded when they watched us catch fish on artificial lures, something they had never seen before. But, as I have mentioned, they surprised us on a later trip by flashing their own handcrafted lures made in imitation of ours.

Our original plan to cruise south only ten miles or so, taking along three skiffs from which to fish once we found game, was greatly altered when an unseasonable norther blustered in. Our mother boat, one of those river launches, couldn't push against the wind. So we cruised with it and went zipping along at a nice speed until we got all the way to the village of Tamiahua at the southern tip of the bay.

Russ Lee of Austin was with us, along with Stagno and Saylor and a couple of other anglers I hadn't met before. We didn't mind being practically blown all the way down into new fishing waters, especially since a tiny stream emptied into the Gulf near the village, and we figured we would murder the snook and tarpon there. We didn't. In fact, we didn't do much good at all—caught enough specks to feed us, which wasn't much to brag about since the trout ranged from six pounds and four would feed the whole gang, including the skipper and his mate. Something was screwball. A beautiful, unfished bay, plenty of grass flats on each side of the channel in the middle of the bay, and a little river connecting the bay and gulf. It should be a fishing paradise.

Felix finally figured it out. Then . . . ah, hang around and listen.

"The tide's going out, isn't it," Felix asked, as we sat on the deck of our mother ship eating breakfast at dawn.

"Sure," I said. "Which means no fishing at the mouth of the river."

"Remember those shrimp traps two or three miles up the bay that we passed on our way down?" Felix asked.

We did.

"Okay. Let's go work 'em over," Felix said.

Those shrimp traps were additional testimony to the inequity of the Mexican fishermen who had not made the complete switch to gringo ways—huge drag seines that clean out a bay in short order. The traps were made in the shape of a "V" with a small opening at the bottom. They were made by pushing green mangrove stems into the muddy bottom. The sticks were so close together that not even shrimp could get through them. The wide part of the "V"-shaped trap started out on the shallow, grassy flat, and the narrow part was tight at the edge of the flat, close to the channel, but still in water no more than four feet deep.

Shrimp moved out over the grass flat at high tide to feed. Then they moved back with the outgoing tide. Some moved into and through the traps. In the daytime it was safe—the Indians did not shrimp in the daytime because the crustaceans could see the tiny net and backtrack, which a shrimp can do in a hell of a hurry. The Indians fished only at night, hanging a kerosene lantern on a peg at the bottom of the trap, and sitting hour after hour, while the tide was moving out, dipping up the shrimp that came through. So we weren't horning in on their fishing, since we went forth in daytime, although they did follow us and watch curiously, some suspiciously, as we began casting lures around their traps.

Felix had figured that if shrimp came through that narrow bottom of the trap when the tide moved out, fish would have enough sense to assemble at the traps and do some feeding. He was right. On my first cast I hung into an eight-pound trout and whipped him down. While I was working him over, Russ, in the boat with me, hung a fifteen-pound snook. I noticed that others in the group were having similar action at other traps.

There it was, dream fishing. Long, lean, silvery snook, ranging from eight to fifteen pounds, specks ranging from three to eight.

The fish were blasting floaters. Since the speckled trout seldom jumps (a hook in the gill will cause him to), I like to get a full measure of enjoyment by making these fish strike at the surface. I might be wrong, but I believe a speck that takes a surface lure will boil at the surface more in fighting the hook. That's what a big speck does—moves up to the surface and jerks his head from side to side. You usually see only a little of his head. But the sound is fine and there is always an element of uncertainty at that moment. Of course, there's always an element of uncertainty when you are fighting a big (four pounds and up) speck, because he has a surprisingly fragile bony structure around his mouth. That's how he got the name weakfish. At any moment the hook might pull through the bone.

It was wild fishing, and we weren't bugged by any small ones. The big ones would have eaten them.

"Who could ask for more?" Russ said.

"I could," I told him.

"What?"

"Tarpon."

"Well, get set, for here they come."

I looked around and saw a three-footer roll—then one a bit larger. When I looked back, I had a tarpon on the line. Schools of them, rather small schools, seemed to have some sort of arrangement as to territorial rights. For they showed up at practically all the traps. They scared the specks away, but not the snook. So we had that delightful combination once more—tarpon and snook. And they were banging away at surface lures.

There was limited commercial fishing at that spot then, mainly because of difficulty getting the fish out. No roads. When it rained—and it rained on us—the dirt roads were impassable. Most of the shrimp caught at those traps was dried. Dried shrimp is fine for those who can stand the stink. I can't seem to negotiate it. So the shrimp take was small—not enough to cut deeply into the food supply for game fish, something that happened at the beautiful Laguna de Terminos, farther south. And there was little commercial fishing. Some fish were dried and sold to nearby ranchers. The nearest large market was Tampico, and it was supplied by fish taken near the city. So our fishing hole was almost virgin—if there can be such a state. And we were sad at the thought of leaving. But time was running out, and when we realized that Old Limp Limp, as we had come to call our mother boat, wasn't going to make it back in the face of the wind, still blowing from the north, we mooched a ride in a truck to a village a dozen miles inland, and there we hired two taxis to take us back to Tampico. And suddenly we came to a halt when we stopped at the little arroyo, where the taxis were ferried across.

The little fellows were ten times livelier than their elders, which I guess you would expect. The instant one felt a hook, it bounced in the air and seemed to stay there, like a marlin "suspended" on a long aerial burst. But we weren't landing any of them—and I wanted to see one on the bank, to examine it and see if it was real. They would hit floaters, but the lures merely bounced.

Finally I dug deep in my tackle box and came up with something I figured might work. It was a lure I had forgotten, a dinky metal thing with some red beads and tiny spinners on it, and treble hooks at the stern so small a minnow could have taken them. It was a lure given to me by a friend in Mexico City when we made a trip way up in the mountains west of there and battled rainbow trout in a little manmade lake. The lure had been made in France, and it was intended for use with spinning gear, which was relatively new then. I could barely cast it. I'm sure it didn't weigh a quarter ounce. But by making a wide swing instead of a quick snap, I could get it out far enough to reach the tarpon.

And I stuck one.

He really put on a dance act as I gently worked him toward the bank, which was eight feet down below me. A little Mexican boy standing in the mud down there grabbed the leader and flipped the twenty-inch baby tarpon up on the shore beside me. Mainly I wanted to feel inside his mouth—to see if the bony structure there was as tough as it is in adult tarpon. It was. I took a couple of photos and put him back in the water. I passed the little lure around and we were having a fine time until somebody said, "We're going to get to Tampico after dark if we don't get moving."

That instantly stopped the fishing. Those blind corners, the dim lights, the wild horn music . . .

I sure didn't want to get caught in that business of competing for the right-of-way at each street intersection. So we hurried on to Tampico and ate rock crabs and broiled pompano, and the next day we headed for the Rio Grande.

"We ought to go back there," I remarked to Felix as we were driving home.

"And take my cartop boat," he said, "and get right down on level with them."

He added, "Then go on up the arroyo, and then down it until it hits the bay."[2]

You plan those trips. You make some. But the range of the tarpon is vast, and you can't make them all.

I never went back to Tampico again. I did, however, resolve that I would find out something about the life cycle of the tarpon. I was merely curious then—and I was still curious after I got the meager available material of a scientific nature on the life cycle of the tarpon. It was vague—and conflicting. So I dropped it.

When I started writing this book, fifteen years after that trip, I felt obliged to go ahead and finish my "research" and really find out about the life cycle of the tarpon. And I quote the word "research," because I never do it personally. I'm allergic to libraries and other gloomy places where you talk in whispers and can't smoke and drink. As I say, fifteen years ago I was merely curious. Now I really wanted to know because of the critical situation in the world of the tarpon, at least along the Texas coast. And before anybody can do anything to help a species survive, somebody must learn about the life cycle of that species.

Know what?

There is no more information available today than there was fifteen years ago. And I was astounded to note the wide variation of "facts" about the tarpon's life cycle in all the bulletins and reports, etc., that I accumulated.

One thing is certain: A female tarpon of good size, 130 pounds or so, will spawn about 12 million eggs. That's a lot of eggs. Another certainty: The eggs hatch into a larval form, a tiny, translucent "flatworm," with two black dots (eyes) at one end. Then the larvae grow "down" instead of up. They absorb whatever stuff is in the larva as they change to a true fish form, like a chicken embryo. Some of my "authorities" say that tarpon spawn from 100 to 200 kilometers out in the open Gulf—or Atlantic—and that the larvae start working their way back toward shore, becoming true fish in the process.

Nuts. I've never seen a tarpon more than twelve miles offshore except around coral islands off Vera Cruz, and those islands are part of a chain, with relatively shallow water between them. Tarpon are not a deepwater fish on the order of sails and dolphin. They are surf and bay and river feeders. But I have seen plenty of those funny translucent things, for Spanish mackerel belch them up now and then when you haul a fish into your boat. I always thought they were the larvae of eels. Maybe they are tarpon in-the-becoming.

Another "authority" says tarpon spawn up rivers.

Another "authority" says they spawn in shallow, muddy bay waters.

Still another says they spawn near inlets where currents will carry the eggs out to sea, way out, then when the eggs hatch, the larval tarpon start working back homeward, angel.

Take your pick of the theories.

All I do know, and I know it definitely, is that the tarpon is an estuarine fish, and that part of the life cycle—probably that of the tiny fish soon after it changes from larval form—is spent in brackish or fresh water. And that tiny fish depends on plankton to survive. Pollute the water, or kill the plankton by running the water through an industrial plant, or stop the flow of water entirely (as in the Rio Grande), and what happens? A link in the life cycle is busted to hell.

Now let's go on to another fishing trip.

# CHAPTER 12

# Landlocked Tarpon

The biggest surprise of my tarpon fishing career came one day when I was serenely casting for black bass in the still, clear water of a resaca near my home in Brownsville. The word resaca is applied to old bends in the Rio Grande but no longer a part of it. The river did a lot of channel cutting and changing in its lower delta before it was harnessed by man. There is no connection between that resaca and the Rio Grande—no way in, no way out. Completely landlocked.

I was fishing alone, something I seldom do. And I got to daydreaming, something I often do, and just sat in the little skiff for a few minutes while my floating lure moved gently up and down with the ripples on the surface. Finally, I solved whatever earth-shaking problem was occupying my mind at the time, and I gave the floater, a plunking-type lure, a gentle nudge. A thirty-inch tarpon latched on and boiled up in the air.

I was so surprised I didn't even try to hit him. I sat staring in utter disbelief as the tarpon rattled his gills. Raising a whale wouldn't have surprised me more. I knew what fish were in that resaca—bass, what we call Rio Grande perch (a cichlid), a dopey fish we call a Mexican sleeper, gars, bream, turtles, mullet, and some odds and ends.

No tarpon. No whales.

Yet there he was, in the act of pitching my lure back at me. I got busy and beat the waters in that entire area, keeping a sharp lookout for any tarpon rolling. Then I made a run up the resaca and down it, going fairly fast and just looking. No signs of another.

When I went to Hurt Batsell's store, fishermen's headquarters, the next

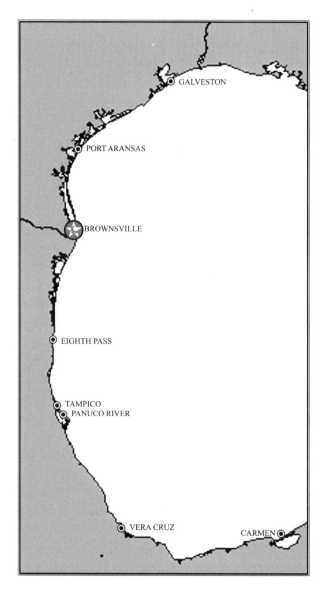

day and told my story, nobody believed me. Hurt was thinking, "The guy's had too much tequila. I told him the stuff was mind softening."

But Hurt did agree to go with me to the resaca the next day and see if we could find my lost tarpon again. Want to guess what we caught? Two snook.

This was too much. Somebody was moving the bay into my resaca (so few other people fished it that I had squatter's rights). Sure, snook go hundreds of miles up rivers, and according to some "authorities" a lot of them never bother to go back and face the rougher life in saltwater. Again I quote the "authorities" because there are none.

The life cycle of the snook is better known than that of the tarpon, but there are still gaps, as, for example, whether the snook can reproduce successfully in landlocked freshwater. The little research done so far has been carried on at the southern tip of Florida—none in southern Mexico and Guatemala and so on, where there are several varieties of snook. Also no research on the Pacific coast of Mexico, where there is a lean, lovely snook that is an exact counterpart of what we call the tide runner on the east coast of Mexico.

Quite obviously at some time in the past snook were able to make their way between the two oceans, since these species are so much alike. But if members of the weakfish tribe ever communicated between two oceans, it sure was a long time ago, since the corbina (sometimes spelled corvina) and totuava of Mexico's west coast are quite different from our old pal the speckled trout of the east coast. Those of the west coast have no spots. And they're larger, which seems true of many kinds of fish—sails, dolphin, etc. As for tarpon—there are none except a few that were lugged across Panama from the Atlantic and planted in the Pacific the past century. Unlike the striped bass, the tarpon has not done much in Pacific waters.

The snook we caught that day were small, about three pounds. And we didn't see a sign of a tarpon. We did, however, figure out how the snook and tarpon got there. During the great hurricane of 1933, which opened all those passes into the Laguna Madre of Mexico, water from the Gulf came inland halfway to Brownsville, and the situation was aggravated by a deluge of twelve inches of rain in twenty-four hours. So those great rollers sweeping inland must have brought tiny snook and tarpon—and the fish somehow managed to get themselves trapped in my resaca when it flooded and met incoming Gulf water.

It was baffling to me then and it is now, mainly because neither I nor any of my fishing companions have ever seen a baby tarpon or snook in the shore waters or rivers of Texas. We took it for granted that these fish did not spawn along the Texas coast. And I still think they do not. Then how come these babies got into my resaca? Probably because the great swells moved in a southeasterly direction, bringing those baby fish from Mexico. I'm not sure. But is any marine biologist ready to come up with a better explanation?

Hurt and Dave and I and several others started a sort of campaign. Catching the two snook convinced Hurt. He didn't doubt my lonesome tarpon story after that. But we weren't having any luck locating that tarpon or any others. And we couldn't catch anymore snook, although now and then some other angler—some "foreigner" horning in on my resaca—would come in with a story about catching a snook or two. Finally we hit pay dirt.

Hurt and I decided to go all the way to the northeast end of the resaca, an area I seldom fished because it wasn't much good for bass. Not enough plant growth in the waters. And we ran smack into a school of about twenty tarpon. We raised four, using bass plunkers, and I landed one. It was thirty-two inches long, sleek, in real fine condition, with no visible signs of damaging fungus or parasites. The school of tarpon vanished after I landed that one—on bass tackle and after a pretty doggone tough hassle—and we couldn't find them again.

Hurt wanted to take the tarpon in and hang it in the entrance to his tackle store. I was reluctant for two reasons: I wanted to leave it there in my resaca so I could catch it again, and I dreaded the thought of an army of strangers storming out to my personal fishing hole in quest of tarpon. But I yielded, so Hurt strung up the fish and put a sign on it saying that I caught it in the Olmito resaca, real name of the resaca.

Fishermen are funny creatures. Nobody showed any interest. In the first place, they thought it was a trick. In the second place, they just weren't interested. Tarpon are no good to eat. We continued fishing the upper part of the resaca—and all other parts of it—but we never raised another tarpon. Never saw one. I caught a couple of snook over a period of six months and noted that they were growing nicely and seemed healthy. Then for almost two years nothing more happened, and we decided the snook and tarpon had died. We were right about the tarpon, wrong about the snook.

One day, during a severe freeze that came near wrecking the citrus fruit industry of the lower Rio Grande Valley, I got a call from a friend who lived on the resaca—at a big bend where there was a deep hole.

"Come on over in a hurry," he said. "Snook are dying."

What he really said was, "Pike are dying." That's what we called the fish when we first encountered it. Later we grudgingly accepted snook as the proper name. That was a sad, sad spectacle. By that time the snook had become man-size. They ranged around ten to fifteen pounds. I've caught much bigger snook, but nobody puts down a ten-pounder. A snook would slowly float to the surface, belly up. Killed by the cold.

"I've counted twenty-one," my friend said, as we stood on the bank shivering in the icy wind, something people in that semitropical country are not accustomed to. What really distressed me was the men in boats out over that deep hole, scooping up snook as they moved up to the surface dead. They were shouting gleefully. Of course, that was the sensible thing to do, since the snook is fine eating—much better than black bass. But at the moment, as I watched those dying snook surface slowly, the men dipping them up seemed like scavengers.

The final "catch" was fifty-four. And as I drove away, I kept thinking, "Where the hell have those snook been for the last year or two? How come I haven't raised one in a year?"

I got the answer later, in trying to catch the snook that snuggle up close to the banks of the Panuco River at Tampico. The snook in my resaca had learned about lures. You confine fish and show them lures for a time and you educate them. Maybe I could have fooled them by offering a live mullet—and the resaca was loaded with mullet. But I don't fish with live—or once live—bait.

You might assume that we could have developed different techniques with a variety of lures and caught some of those snook, just as we always managed to catch tarpon one way or another if we were among them. But the situations are not parallel. Tarpon gather in certain spots—inlets, deep holes in bays, deep holes in rivers, the mouth of rivers, etc.—and you can see them. Finally, you work out a trick of some kind to get action, even if the tarpon have been fished hard for quite a spell. But snook? You don't know where they are. And who wants to work miles and miles of shoreline trying to trick something that isn't there?

What we considered doing was arranging to have several thousand small snook and tarpon dumped in the resaca. We talked to a lot of people about the idea, but the reaction was pretty negative. Federal and state agencies just weren't interested—had no funds allocated for the project, and they didn't think much of the idea anyway.

We learned that we could probably have some small snook and tarpon caught in seines in some bay in Mexico, then put in tanks and flown to Brownsville. But that involved quite a bit of clams—and nobody had any money at that time, the middle of the Big Depression. Hurt and Dave and I were thinking of doing the job ourselves—driving to Tampico, arranging for commercial fishermen to catch small tarpon and snook with seines, and lugging them back in tanks. The jostling on that rough road would be enough to properly aerate the water for snook—and tarpon don't need much aerating since they take in a lot of air.

But about that time the Brownsville Ship Channel was started, and here came the snook and redfish and big speckled trout and small tarpon, following the dredge as it cut its way inland. The fishing in the new channel was so good that we forgot about our landlocked snook and tarpon venture.

Now—after a time span of more than thirty years, the idea comes back to mind. And it takes on new and far more significant impact as I watch the spectacle of man moving the striped bass inland—into landlocked fresh water lakes. I'll play around with that idea later, after I'm through fishing. Right now let's make a run at some waters that offered still another kind of tarpon fishing.

# CHAPTER 13

## Manmade Tarpon Holes

It is difficult to imagine finding something new in tarpon fishing after twenty years of ranging the home waters of this fish. But I found something new, and only a hundred miles from my home at the time, Houston. It would be better to say that I was led to this new kind of fishing by Felix Stagno, Houston guitar player and tackle salesman who was a fishing companion of mine at the time.

If the combination of guitar player and tackle salesman seems a bit unusual, go to Houston and check on other combinations of abilities in an effort to survive. Musicians in Houston are paid peanuts—about the same as newspapermen. So you run into a fine sax man who sells hurricane fences on the side, and a talented piano man who sells organs, which he hates.

That new fishing hole was the New Brazos, as the stretch of the Brazos River near the Gulf of Mexico is called. And people don't say New Brazos River—just New Brazos. It is a manmade channel, a straight-line cut about six miles inland from the Gulf. Tarpon were rolling there, and they came in what I considered the proper catching sizes, three to four feet. Fine on the light casting tackle we used in speckled trout fishing.

Felix started the seven-horse motor latched onto the stern panel of his ten-foot, canvas-covered cartop boat, and we cruised out near the tarpon, cut the motor, and drifted with the wind, near enough to reach them. We were using our "floating spoons," which I have mentioned before—three-eighths-ounce metal spoons that we could make bounce and ski and gurgle along the surface. We would let a spoon dip into the water now and

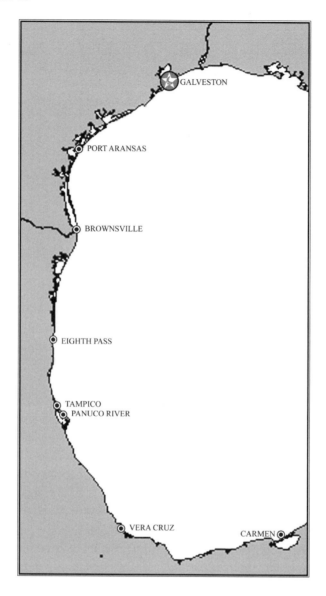

then, producing a juicy gurgling sound as if something were dying. Fish love things in the process of dying—can't run away or fight back.

Both of us cast, something we never do if the tarpon are in the five- to six-foot class. We take it one at a time then, for the man who hangs such a tarpon is likely to need help in a hurry, mainly a chasing job with the motor at full rev. The three-footers were no threat—just a prospective joy.

We got strikes. I lost mine but Felix stuck his, and after a lively fight of about fifteen minutes he brought it alongside and we eased out the little hook and released the fish. Then I hung one. I didn't really need help, but Felix kept the motor running slowly, mainly with the idea of taking flight if the tarpon headed toward our boat. I lost the tarpon, but soon we were both latched onto others—and so it went. The perfect tarpon hole. And man had created it. God bless man until the ugly aftereffects of his handiwork become obvious. Now and then man does something that seems really fine—such as that tarpon hotspot. Sadly, it seems that "tarpon shalt not long endure." All too often what man does is undone—or he wishes that he could undo it.

That straight channel is nine feet deep and about two hundred yards wide. It was cut to prevent flooding around the town of Freeport, south of Houston, and to better provide the needs of petrochemical plants in that area. It was fairly new when I first fished it—still had plenty of appeal to tarpon, which meant that food-bearing water was running—or creeping—down from the main river, attracting mullet and shrimp and other things that attract tarpon.

A new channel being dredged inland from the sea causes tarpon and many other gamefishes to act crazy, as I knew from fishing right behind the huge dredge that was cutting the Brownsville Ship Channel, back in the mid-1930s. I'll tell you about that a bit later. In such a channel as the New Brazos, tarpon deviate sharply from the pattern you accept as normal in waters not disturbed by man. In the New Brazos there was no deep channel—there is in natural streams flowing into the sea. So no holes had been washed out by the current changing from side to side. The bottom was level, nine feet from bank to bank. The channel was in a straight line, something you do not find in nature.

Flow from the river, controlled way up the line and doled out in puny amounts, was not enough to cut a channel. In fact, much of the water in the New Brazos moves back and forth with the tide. As a result, a school of tarpon seldom remained in one spot very long. We moved with them. At one place, near the south shore of the river, we got set to move when tarpon abandoned us—but not all of them did, as Felix discovered to his confusion. Before starting the motor, he put his rod down on the stern panel. The spoon he was using was dangling in the water. I always fasten my lure to my reel when I am not fishing—but every man is entitled to his own pattern of handling his gear. As the motor started, the spoon came to the surface, about six feet behind the boat, and began wobbling. And a tarpon blasted it. Pretty doggone wild for a couple of minutes, as Felix tried to cut off the motor and grab his rod all at the same time. But the tarpon kicked free.

The tarpon seemed to be confused. They seemed to be hunting here and there for a deep hole, a channel wash, a concentration of prey food. Since there were no big concentrations, the fish kept cruising about, running into small schools of prey food, then moving on again. So we moved with them. We worked over the travelers, those tarpon obviously on the move from one spot to another. And did a neat job. As I recall it, we boated six tarpon, all under four feet, and were about to call it a day (we never bother to fish after noon) when along came a monster on the move.

"Take him," Felix said.

"After you, my dear Alphonse," I said. Sure, I would have gotten a kick out of a blast from the big fellow—and no man ever deliberately passes up a tarpon, no matter how big the fish or how frail the tackle. But that was late in my tarpon career, whereas Felix, even though he had done far more fishing for speckled trout than I and was an expert in light tackle, had done relatively little tarpon fishing. One hooked now and then while fishing in some bay or on an occasional trip to an inlet. Let him battle it.

The tarpon was heading for the mouth of the river. Felix decided he would let me have the honor of dedicating a lure to the tarpon, so he cruised parallel to the monster so I could flip the spoon out in front of it. I put the spoon about four feet in front of his nose just as he rolled—and he latched on. And when he fell back to the water after a jump, he headed for the sea, which wasn't too far away.

Felix opened up the motor and got the little boat planing, so we could stay with the tarpon on the first big run. But my leader was only two feet long, and I knew the tiny treble hooks on the spoon wouldn't take much gumming from the tarpon. Then . . . then, even though Felix was urging me to hang on, I heard the rumbling of the surf and felt the first swell gently lift the boat. A bit farther out, there would be nothing gentle about the manner in which those swells would lift that frail craft. I clamped down and let the tarpon have the spoon.

And as Felix came about and headed upstream, there was a cracking sound from stem to stern and suddenly the bottom of that boat came bulging on up even with the rail, something no boat bottom should do. The ribs of the boat, rotted by years of being soaked in the water and not entirely dried out, cracked along the little keel. But the boat held together as we limped on up the river to our starting point.

The New Brazos wasn't (and I use the past tense now since tarpon are gone from it) nearly as oddball as many other manmade channels and lakes that I have fished, although it did present a kind of tarpon fishing that was new to me, even after more than twenty years of pursuing the silver king. Any time man creates a new fishing spot, freshwater or saltwater, strange and often delightful things are certain to happen.

In the Era of the Dam, most freshwater fishermen know just how sensational a new lake can be—and they learn how the "life cycle" of the lake is likely to be capsulated into a span of not more than ten years. I've fished many such lakes, some huge, some small. I've fished them when they were brand new, when they were middle-aged, and when they were in the process of decay, insofar as fishing was concerned.

When a dam is built and water moves out over land, the abundance of life, much of it microscopic, causes seeming miracles to happen, as little fish and crustaceans move out over the land, then big gamefish move out in pursuit of the smaller creatures. Fish grow at an astonishing rate—perhaps three or four times what is considered normal. And they usually strike as though each lure flung at them would be the last. They seem to lack caution, probably because of limited experience in dealing with lures.

I've caught big bass grazing around clumps of partially submerged prickly pear in a new lake near the Rio Grande—cactus bass, you could call them. And I've hauled fine fighting bass out from the interior of some old home partially submerged by rising waters of a new lake. I've fished Texoma, a big lake on the Texas–Oklahoma line, and caught big bass fishing over what we called "Aunt Maggie's Peach Orchard." We could see the tops of the submerged peach trees. Bass are caught on submerged railroad tracks—and at other dopey places. I've encountered them at lakes in Mexico, such as Don Martin, and at dozens of lakes in this country.

But that cycle . . . it seems inevitable. The rise, glory, and decline, as of the Roman Empire, but during a capsuled time span. And after ten or fifteen years many of these fine new lakes are pretty punk fishing. Some are even "killed," as aquatic biologists call it, and started new. The revived lake is seldom comparable to the original.

In contrast, the natural lakes seem to hold up, although it is true that as fishing becomes more concentrated, the fish learn more. So among the best lakes in Texas to this day is Caddo, on the Texas–Louisiana line. And it can hardly be called a natural lake now, since the retaining dam, once a natural obstacle, is being boosted now and then, raising the lake level. Well, you find a similar situation when you move down to the sea in pursuit of tarpon and other saltwater gamefish.

The wildest fishing I can recall, except the Eighth Pass and Carmen in Mexico, was in the Brownsville Ship Channel while it was being dredged. But for reasons which still puzzle me, it never could be considered a really top tarpon spot—schools now and then, but not predictable. That's why, twenty years later, I was surprised to find lively fishing for tarpon in the New Brazos.

But when that Brownsville Ship Channel was being dredged, smack across dry land ten feet above sea level, the things that happened were sort of miraculous in the world of the speckled trout, redfish, snook, and even flounder. And the fishing held up for almost ten years, partly because oil did not figure in the early operations of the port, and even dry cargo traffic was puny—a couple of freighters a week. And there was no DDT then.

This was in sharp contrast to most other ship channels dredged in the country—or perhaps I should say deepened, because they were channels or canals of some sort before being dredged deeper.

A tremendous amount of tiny plant and animal life must have been loosened by the dredge as it cut inland, and for several years the drain off from the relatively flat land, through drainage canals, brought still more plant and animal life in minute form. At any rate, crustaceans and tiny fish follow the dredge inland, and larger fish followed them—and we followed the dredge. We sort of haunted it, for the best fishing, as you might expect, was in or along the line between clear and murky water, near the dredge.

Looking back, I am puzzled most by the sudden blossoming of spectacular snook fishing. The only snook we had seen prior to dredging of the channel were in Mexico. We didn't even call them snook—they were "pike" to us, because of that underslung lower jaw. Suddenly they were swarming in the channel—and they began using that as a sort of base, spreading on out into the bay waters. Everybody was delighted, particularly the commercial fishermen who were dragging seines (illegally) in the bay.

Why did those snook suddenly cross the Rio Grande because of that channel? I know a few snook are taken farther north along the Texas coast. But only a loner now and then, whereas millions of them moved into the

Laguna Madre north of the Rio Grande when the channel was built. And all were large—from seven to eight pounds up. I never saw a small snook north of the Rio Grande, just as I never saw a baby tarpon north of it. And another kind of fish came breezing in—the skipjack.

Like the tarpon, the skipjack is not considered a food fish. And like the tarpon, it leaps when hooked—it goes wild. If skipjacks averaged four pounds instead of less than two, they would be great gamefish. And in some parts of tropical waters—such as Carmen—they do average close to four pounds. Most anglers avoid them. I like them. And I had plenty to give me action for several years after the ship channel at Brownsville was dredged. Then they sort of fizzled out. The fish that we call a skipjack is usually called a tenpounder or ladyfish in Florida, where many show up. Both names sound a bit silly, since a ten-pounder would be a freak and half the fish are gentlemen, not ladies. But it's okay with me. All I'm curious about is the sudden appearance of great schools of pretty fair-sized skipjacks just as the ship channel was being finished, then the fadeout of the fish.

Snook lingered around longer, but most of those that did hid under the docks in the turning basin and refused to strike lures. Got smart, like the snook along the banks of the Panuco. These moved when traffic in oil began fouling up the water—that is, most of them moved. Some waited too long and were killed by cold during one of the rare prolonged hard freezes in that area.

I guess the flounder had been there all along, since you catch (mainly by spearing) them all along the Gulf coast. All the channel did was cause them to concentrate—and to strike lures. We really couldn't get lures to them in the shallow flats where they usually bedded down to wait for food. In the channel we could. We trolled until one hit, then stopped and cast. Real nice fishing for a few years, until age set in and the channel grew weary.

The glory days of tarpon fishing in the Brownsville Channel were even briefer. Schools moved in and out when the channel was new. Now and then we would see them and get some action. But nothing to compare with the New Brazos twenty years later. At the time we figured the ship traffic scared tarpon out of the channel. There is no ship traffic in the New Brazos. Maybe we were wrong. I'll let somebody else figure out why they moved into the Brownsville Ship Channel, took a look for a time, then departed, especially since snook, with habits much the same as the tarpon, stayed for a long time.

# CHAPTER 14

# Rollers on the Rocks

A big swell would lift our sixteen-foot outboard rig high in the air, then deposit us in the trough, eight or ten feet lower. Then another wave. And a mere forty yards away were the twenty-ton granite blocks that formed the jetty. Rollers ran on into them, after slipping under us, then—CRASH! And spray flew over the few anglers stupid enough to stand on the rocks and fish.

Understand why I've done little fishing around jetties?

But the tarpon were there, big fellows, and for some dopey reason—maybe hometown loyalty—Dave and I considered it our duty to fish for those tarpon so that we might make a contribution to the Port Isabel Tarpon Rodeo—the second one to be staged.

I have been assured by physicists that waves do not cause water to move horizontally unless they crest—or are near land, in which case rollers move inland a bit, then pile up water as they wash back. So even if waves are not cresting, the water level along a surf will be higher than the level miles out to sea. If waves are mighty and cresting, which happens when a hurricane drives the water, then the tide along shore may rise eight or ten feet. But normal waves are just water moving up and down, the physicists tell me. Same effect as that on air when sound waves move through it—no horizontal movement of the air.

But you try to sell that story to a couple of guys in a light boat being bounced around by big but noncresting rollers and see how much luck you have.

"I don't like it worth a damn," I told Dave.

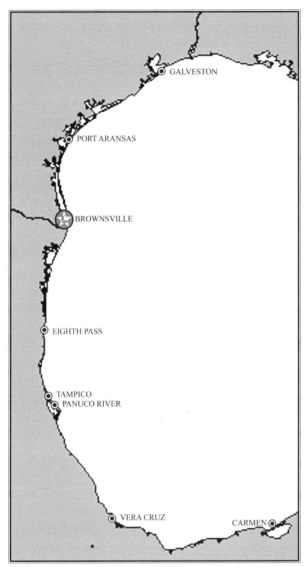

"I don't either," he said. "If we can't hang one in a few minutes, let's get the hell away from these rocks."

So Dave hung one in a hurry.

Dave banged his monster plug, one made for muskies, against a rock, and it dropped near a tarpon, which immediately latched on. In those days, 1936–39, no really good tarpon plugs were being made. So in the rodeo, because we really were anxious to land any big fish we hung, Dave and I used what would be considered light surf tackle—a reel that held more than 250 yards of nine-thread linen line (27-pound test) and long rods. We had to use a heavy plug to cast with that gear.

I headed away from the jetty as soon as Dave stuck the six-foot tarpon, and we had a noble battle. Remember, that was in the early days of my tarpon fishing, when actually boating a six-footer was a big event—for me as well as for the rodeo promoters. But we paid the penalty of using leaders only two feet long. The tarpon, after a twenty-minute battle, managed to roll up in the line and cut it back of the leader. The man who trolls near the rocks has a big advantage—he can use a six- or seven-foot leader. You can't cast with that kind of leader, especially if you're squatting down in a little boat being bounced in waves. And if you must troll, I'd rather make the hop to Mexico's Pacific coast, where I can take billfish—and occasionally big dolphin and big roosterfish. And you don't have to continue trolling if you hang a big dolphin or roosterfish. They usually move in big schools, so you can stop and cast, once you get a strike.

The wind began picking up and we noticed some of the rollers were beginning to feather at the top. So we abandoned the jetty. Anyway, Dave and I had something better in mind, something I'll explain in detail in the next chapter, for it concerns a kind of trickery in fishing that might help anglers in many situations—even on bass and crappie.

But I've been back to the rocks again and again—always because of somebody else, not because I wanted to catch big tarpon there. And I've fished smack in the surf where the rollers were curling over and crashing—because somebody else wanted to fish there. So maybe I should at least tell a few of the highlights.

I got a call one day from Peter Barrett, outdoors editor of *True Magazine*, for which I was writing regularly at the time. Pete and Emmett Gowen, another outdoor writer, had gone to Port Aransas, Texas, as guests of the people in what was once called the Tarpon Capital of the World. But they had gone to fish for billfish, not tarpon. The billfish boom was underway then—and the tarpon boom on its way out. The Port Aransas Tarpon Rodeo had been changed to the Port Aransas Deep Sea Roundup.

It was still pretty good tarpon fishing spot when Pete called me. But that was about sixteen years ago, and tarpon fishing along much of the coast ranged from fair to punk. The decline had set in.

"Our hosts are killing us with kindness," Pete told me, "but we're not catching any fish."

"What are you fishing for?" I asked. I didn't even know Pete and Emmett were at Port Aransas.

"We've been roaming the Gulf fifty miles out trying to raise sails and marlin," Pete said. "Got a fine offshore cruiser, but it is rough as hell out there and we haven't seen fish."

"They're out there," I said. "Just hard to see them when the water's rough."

"Well, we want to switch to something we can see," Pete said. "Plenty of tarpon around the end of the jetties and in the surf. How about coming down and helping us?"

I was living in Houston at the time.

"There are dozens of people there who know more about tarpon fishing than I'll ever know," I told Pete. "See Barney Farley. He's the grandpa of the guides—the best."[1]

What I didn't tell him was that I don't give a damn for tarpon fishing around jetties or in the surf. Pete insisted, so I drove on down and was astounded when those two wild men insisted that we breeze out through the pass and fish the surf right then—close to noon.

"That pass is rugged for little boats after the wind comes up," I said. Along the Gulf coast you can usually expect the wind to start building up around 9 or 10 in the morning. "And the surf's sure rough."

"I got a boat that can take it," Emmett said.

And he did have a really fine rig—a 22-foot boat with a 60-horsepower outboard latched onto it. So I said okay, let's go get swamped or rolled up in a swell, if that's what they wanted. If you're going to fish the surf from a boat, you've got to get right in as close to shore as possible in order to reach the fish. Breaking waves cause a lot of commotion—if the water is clear you can sometimes see mullet or trout or redfish racing along in a swell as it rises and thins out before spilling over. And we saw tarpon—big ones.

Pete's gear wasn't worth a hoot for casting, and Emmett's wasn't much better. I don't think either of them had done much tarpon fishing before. So I took the motor and handed my gear to Pete. He got off a nice cast, fairly close to a couple of tarpon. When he didn't get action, he began reeling the lure in rapidly—and a monster blasted into it right smack at the stern of the boat, less than six feet away. All of a sudden I could see Pete "listening" to some of the things I had written for *True*. He hung two more big ones, way out near the end of his cast, but they shook loose.

Emmett wasn't having much luck, so he kept urging me to get in close to the breakers. He couldn't cast far enough with his rig. I suggested an alternative—change rigs with Pete. Use mine.

I've had some experiences in those breakers that I do not intend to repeat. I've fished the surf with a couple of madmen—but I never go out with the same madman twice, and you can't always tell in advance. A couple of years before our trip I was fiddling around just outside the breakers with just such a madman. I'll call him Buckshot, which wasn't his name—and, incidentally, it is only the second phony name used in this book. All the others are real.

Buckshot talked me into working the surf for tarpon and other fish because he is a fine piano man, and I am such a music buff that I can't turn down a musician. He was running the boat—his boat.

I kept trying to get him to stay outside the swells before they started building up to the inevitable crash landing. Buckshot wasn't hearing my kind of music. Madman. So I cast at a tarpon I saw in a roller that was in the process of building up, and the tarpon was gentleman enough to latch on. Out of the corner of my eye I saw Buckshot getting ready to cast! He was steering the boat with his left foot as he stood up to cast.

"Don't cast!" I shouted.

I was too late. He hung a tarpon and started yelling and whopping—and forgot about the motor. Wind whipped the bow around toward shore and as we went racing in toward land a big wave crashed over us, swamping the boat. Up onto the sand—and another wave crashed over us. You won't believe what Buckshot did, not even if you had seen it. The idiot hung a tarpon (I lost mine in the confusion), and the minute the boat grounded he climbed out and began following the fish along the shore, paying no attention to me or the boat.

You can beat down a really big tarpon in the surf if you have about three hundred yards of line, even if it is quite light. For a hooked tarpon is extremely reluctant to get outside the rollers for fear of sharks. Buckshot whipped that one down.

I bailed out the boat and sat waiting for him. We managed to get the craft through the breakers and back into the surf, whereupon I took the motor and told Buckshot I would be his guide from then on. I stayed away from the breakers—and never fished with Buckshot again.

Pete and Emmett are quite reasonable and sensible about fishing, and the trip with them was enjoyable but too short. When I refused to get too close to the breakers, they understood. And the following day we set forth with the "Guiding Hand," venerable Barney Farley, along with us, in his own small but quite adequate offshore cruiser.

Barney was way along in years then. He achieved fame because he was the guide standing beside President Franklin D. Roosevelt and the big tarpon, back in the mid-1930s. He went out with us as a sort of accommodation, for he had quit active guiding. And, of course, Emmett and Pete got the kind of action they had come to get. And they got it at the spot that I disliked even more than the surf—over the submerged rocks at the end of the huge rock jetty.

If there are any tarpon near an inlet that has jetties, the surest spot is right at the tip, where water dislodges and cracks (yes, I mean cracks) some of the big stones during storms. But . . . if you cast there, you are almost certain to eventually hang one of those submerged rocks. And if you troll around the point, you get banged by crosscurrents and crisscross waves.

You can have it.

I saw Pete once after that, in New York. And saw Emmett several years later, when he stopped in Houston on his way south to set up a fishing operation on an island near the border of Mexico and Guatemala. Last I heard he was doing fine.

Although fishing from a jetty is not my brand of booze, I'll tell you something about it. I guess I should try to avoid gaps in the story of tarpon fishing. I have, on about a dozen occasions, fished from the top of jetties for tarpon. It's a nice way to slowly melt down. Tarpon come to the Texas coast in the spring and leave in the fall. They're warm weather fish. So you stand on sizzling rocks in a blazing sun and cast.

When you hang a tarpon, chances are you can whip him down if you have 250 yards of line, and it doesn't have to be heavy line. For the fish is likely to stay reasonably close to the rocks, and all you need do is stay parallel with him and slowly work him down. The tarpon goes out to the end of the jetty, rounds the point, comes back a way on the other side, then goes through the same routine again. Like a tarpon hooked in the surf, he seldom ventures far out. Probably fear of sharks and porpoise. And if you insist on using "porpoises" as the plural, which Mr. Webster advises, go right ahead. Mr. Webster also lists "tarpons" as the plural of tarpon. You say "tarpons" to a fisherman and he'll think you're out of your cotton-picking mind.

Marine biologists say that porpoise do not feed on tarpon—that they feed almost exclusively on menhaden, at least in my part of the world. I never argue with marine biologists. I just put down here what I have seen—at least a dozen tarpon killed by porpoise. Maybe the porpoise are killing for fun, and it really seems that way at times, since a porpoise is likely to bounce a tarpon in the air for a bit before cutting it in two. I doubt that fun business. Only *Homo sapiens* kill for fun. I have a hunch that a mountain lion, forced to leap on a big buck deer to ease severe hunger, thinks, "What a crummy break, getting my ribs banged in by those big antlers. Why the hell didn't a fawn or a sick doe come along?"

Anyway, you follow your tarpon, putting on pressure all the time until he turns on his side, the signal of defeat. What do you do then?

Me, I break loose, for the only safe, sane way to land the fish is to guide it all the way back to the surf, maybe a half mile away, and beach it, something I won't do. If you go down on those rocks to take out the hooks or to get your tarpon and lug it back as a symbol of victory, you're really inviting disaster. Those rocks are slippery. So I make you a present of jetty fishing for tarpon and move on to something more to my liking.

# CHAPTER 15

# Where the Twain Shall Meet

If you had watched Hurt Batsell and me that day, you might have concluded that we had been in the sun too long. Casting lures into water so soupy that a self-respecting mud turtle would abandon it. How could a fish that feeds by sight, not smell, locate a lure in that muddy water? But if you had hung around for a spell, you would have understood the logic of our "mud casting." For you would have noticed what we were looking for—a big silvery fish flash out of the muddy water, leaving below him a "hole" of clear blue water.

I know it sounds nutty. But anglers often pass up surprisingly fine fishing because they do not devote enough thought and study and experimenting to the things that happen when clear water and muddy water meet. And I mean horizontally or vertically or slantwise. Take your choice. Muddy water pouring out of the Rio Grande and clear blue water of the Gulf had both a horizontal and vertical relationship the day Hurt and I were fishing the mud. We started the day in search of king mackerel, which Texans usually call kingfish. Quite a few other fishermen were there, trolling along the line, clearly but irregularly defined, where muddy water and clear water met. The line was shoved this way and that by waves and wind, so it was quite irregular. But clearly defined.

River water moving northward, because of the rather light Gulf current (not the Gulf Stream) at that point. And as the river water moved northward, it fanned out, finally fading away five or six miles northeast of the mouth of the river.

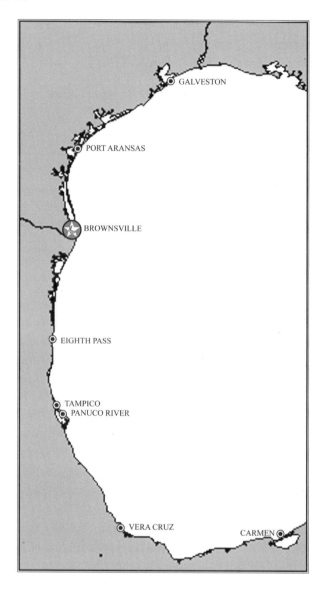

The other anglers were trolling in the clear water but near the line and catching plenty of kings. Hurt and I would troll until we had a strike, then stop and cast. The kings, which ranged from five to twenty pounds, put up a real fine battle, and they hit the lures freely, although our arms were wearing out because we had to retrieve so fast.

We followed the line on toward the mouth of the Rio Grande, then we noticed some action about a hundred yards from the line—in the murky water. Tarpon were rolling. It was difficult to believe. That was in the early days of our tarpon fishing, and we had never seen the silver king in water so murky that a plug four inches away could be invisible. The tarpon were doing more than merely rolling. Now and then one would strike—and we saw one bounce a mullet in the air on the strike.

All of a sudden we abandoned the king mackerel to their fate and cruised out in the soupy water. As we did, I looked back and saw that the prop of the outboard was churning up clear water. There was only a layer, probably six or eight inches thick, of muddy freshwater lying on top of the blue Gulf water. It takes time for freshwater running into a bay or gulf to be assimilated into the saltwater, which is heavier.

Well, mullet, which frequently hunt murky water for protection against predators, were fiddling around in that six or eight inches of river water, and tarpon were down below them, waiting for a fin to show. All very nice—except that we got absolutely no action during a half hour of fishing. We tried floaters. Nothing. And various lures that dug down. Still nothing. Then I recalled a trick Dave Young used several years before to take fish when he and I were casting into the Rio Grande near its mouth. There was a thin film of murky water on top of the clear water—but no thick layer of really soupy water such as Hurt and I encountered out in the Gulf.

When Dave and I wore our arms off casting without getting a strike, he finally reversed the little metal "bib" at the front end of his lure, the gadget put there to make the lure dig down and wobble. We were using lures made for king mackerel—first really good tarpon lures we had been able to get. So Dave would cast out and reel in rapidly, keeping the lure at or close to the surface, although part of it, mainly the tail hooks, would flash just below the film of murky water now and then.

We got wild action.

Hurt and I were either working lures in the muddy water, which meant that tarpon couldn't see them, or letting the lures dig down below that film and be clearly visible in the crystal clear blue water. Tarpon are not suckers. Once a lure dug down below the film, they could see that it wasn't a mullet. So I reversed the bib or lip on my lure. It took a bit of experimenting to bring the lure in so that the tail hooks would flash below the film now and then. Then it was bingo! And bingo! And BINGO! Hurt thought it was pretty dopey—until he reversed the bib on his plug and hung a five-footer. That converted him.

I'm going to digress for a moment and pass along to anglers a few fundamentals in fishing where waters of a different kind—fresh and salt, murky and clear, etc.—meet. And I talk about other fish as well as tarpon. It is at such meeting in places that the finest of all fishing is likely available, if the angler will study the situation and make adjustments. Most people, even the so-called experts, are likely to go through the same old routine. And sometimes be greatly embarrassed when some novice has fine luck simply because he does the unexpected—for example, those dumb fisher-men at the Eighth Pass who showed us how to catch snook because they were punk at casting and had backlashes.

Since the switch from regular casting tackle to spinning gear threatens to eliminate the backlash from fishing, we can ignore it as a "technique" for taking fish. But you can experiment even if you don't have backlashes. Probably the most freakish experience I ever had in using what seemed to be a nutty technique took place on the Brownsville Ship Channel four or five years after it was dredged, when its days of glory were beginning to fade. And small tarpon figured in that experience, along with snook and trout—my kind of trout (saltwater), not rainbows. Seeing tarpon sur-prised me—they seldom showed in the channel at that time.

We had been told that fish assembled at a point where there was a small flow of water into the channel from a drain ditch. The drain ditches car-ried off excess irrigation water, so there was quite a bit of life in the water. We were also told that the fish would not strike.

Of course we didn't believe that, just as Hurt didn't believe Dave and me when we told him that the tarpon in the big bend of the Rio Grande would take nothing but plugs on the bottom. So we set forth, determined to make those fish strike. We didn't. At least not for an hour. It was mad-dening. Big specks would plop at the surface, snook would slash, and now and then a small tarpon—catching size—would blast. They completely ignored our lures, even though we used everything we had, at the surface and below it.

We had just got a new kind of lure, one which seemed worthless to us. It was a small—three-eighths-ounce—plug that had practically no action, regardless how you worked it. No bib under the snout—not even a notch. Just a piece of painted wood vaguely resembling a tiny fish in shape. Since nothing else worked, I tied on one of the things.

We stood about twelve feet above the water level, since the bank was elevated at the drain ditch. So I cast beyond the feeding fish and brought the lure in fast, making no attempt to give it action. I just had it skimming along the surface with the tiny tail hooks flashing down below the thin layer of fresh, and slightly murky, water coming out of the drain ditch. I had four strikes on that one cast. Fish miss a lure at the surface moving that fast. But on the next cast I hung a five-pound speck, and Hurt and Dave quickly tied on similar lures and soon we were in business.

Why?

For the same reason that Hurt and I hung those tarpon under the layer of muddy fresh water off the mouth of the Rio Grande. We were showing the trout and snook and tarpon a momentary flash of the tail hooks now and then as the lure raced along. It served. And when I began watching more carefully, I realized why. From time to time a school of tiny fish—I do not know what kind—would come out of the drain ditch, where they had been feeding, and make a mad dash for the other side of the ship channel, where the murky water was being driven by the wind. When those little fellows came out, there was action. And we managed to duplicate it. We missed most of our strikes but wound up with a total of only six snook, real nice ones; eight specks; and two small tarpon. We had scored a moral victory. We made those fish strike.

Those experiences and others convince me that anglers can make "inland" tarpon and snook strike, if these fine game fish are ever brought inland, something I have talked about and will mention again before I sign off. I don't believe those landlocked tarpon and snook in my pet resaca at Brownsville could whip me down now the way they did more than thirty years ago. Dave and Hurt and I got action at the mouth of that drain ditch because we duplicated the action of the tiny fish on which the gamefish were feeding. You get action where the waters meet—if you know how. I've caught white bass that way when I couldn't take them any other way. And black bass at the mouth of a tiny creek. And huge rainbow trout way up in a mountain lake in Mexico where a dinky stream lazily edged into the lake.

Quite often you get a reverse situation if the waters meet horizontally, or slantwise, instead of vertically. Then you may have to cast into clear water and nudge your lure into murky water. You find that situation often when bay and gulf waters, both salty, meet.

That was the problem Dr. Dean and Bink Goodrich and I faced when we managed to hang tarpon and snook at Carmen. It was the situation when Dan Holland and the rest of us hung all those snook and tarpon at the Eighth Pass. I think the most unusual example of action where bay and gulf waters meet took place on a trip Russell Lee of Austin and I made to Port Aransas, back when the silver king's glory was barely tarnished.

Russ and I have made many fishing trips together, although mostly freshwater, which he prefers. But there have been saltwater trips, especially some memorable jaunts far down the Baja California peninsula in Mexico—back in the days when sportfishing was relatively new there. I got word that tarpon were pretty active in a little cove just inside the south jetty at Port Aransas. They could be reached by casting—and from the sandy beach, not the burning hot jetties—I was told. So Russ and I made a run there, and he was properly excited, since tarpon fishing was new to him then.

This little cove may be gone now. I don't know. The contours of the shore in and around the passes changes, sometimes as a result of hurricanes. But in earlier days quite a few records for tarpon fishing—most in a day by one angler—were set and broken in or near that cove. I've forgotten exact figures, but it seems to me one angler landed seventeen tarpon in a day. And I mean big ones around six feet.

It was the general practice then to take a scale from a tarpon and release him. So along the walls of the famed Tarpon Inn were hundreds of tarpon scales—"trophies"—with the name of the angler and the date and the weight of the fish. Of course those tremendous catches were made by fishermen using huge tackle and trolling mullet. You could whip a six-footer down in ten minutes—even less if the boatman did a little dragging, which he usually did. And the record catches were made back in the days when only a few "crazy people" fished for tarpon. A man trying to set a record was practically certain to have the show all to himself. Throw fifty other anglers into the scramble and see how many tarpon one person might catch.

Russ and I got there at exactly the right time—tarpon action in that cove, and they were near enough for us to reach from shore. But—the same old sad sack story. They wouldn't strike. So we began studying the situation. We walked to the base of the jetty and saw that schools of mullet were moving through the inlet and into the bay. But when they rounded the point of land beyond which the tide had scoured out the cove, they would make a wild dash across the cove to achieve safety in shallow water on the other side of it—up the bay a bit.

"We'll do what they're doing," I suggested to Russ.

So we cast out, right in the middle of a school of mullet rounding the point, and let the fast tide rip carry our lures, nudging them a bit to keep pace with the mullet. As the plugs came around the point, they moved from clear gulf water into bay water slightly murky because the tide rip scoured the sandy bottom. And as the plugs moved—the silver kings struck.

Several tarpon we hung were too big to check. They just went right on out in the bay, flapping a final goodbye at the end of the line. Or just before the end. Never again do I let a big fish run off all my line. But we landed four tarpon in the five-foot class, which was plenty of adventure for Russ and a lot of fun for me.

I think about that trip, and about the others that called for unusual techniques, because the tarpon fishermen of the future is going to be forced to learn a lot more about the ways of this great game fish if he expects to hang one now and then. And, of course, we are rapidly approaching a situation in which a man might say, with pride, "I caught a big tarpon once," just as a man might have said, twenty years ago, "I shot a lion." But before the mourning session, let's make one more trip to a spot where there were plenty of tarpon—but they wouldn't strike.

# CHAPTER 16

# Farewell to the Rio Grande

I followed the trail of the silver king for ten years after my farewell to the Rio Grande.

But I choose to wind up the action part of this book with an account of that last trip, mainly because of the memories the trip brought back—memories of the beginning and events along the way to the end. It was a last trip in more ways than one.

It was my last tarpon fishing trip with Dave and Hurt. All of us knew that, although nothing was said about it at the time—except that the days of glory of tarpon fishing in the Rio Grande were drawing to a close.

I phoned Dave from Houston, where I was living at the time, and arranged the trip. He said there were plenty of tarpon in what we called the Highway Bend, but added, "They won't strike."

"I guess I don't need to ask why . . ."

"The turistas," Dave said. "Tarpon struck fine for three or four weeks after they came into the river. But with twenty or thirty boats out at every hole—they finally quit."

"Well, I'd just like to see them roll," I said. "Anyway, I want to go across the river and get some cabrito¹ and guacamole and tequila . . ."

"I'll arrange it," Dave said.

We went across the river to Matamoros and had cabrito and guacamole and tequila at our old stand, The Texas Bar. Of course Hurt didn't go with us. He won't eat cabrito and he doesn't drink. Even the tequila brought back memories—from way back, when I was in my teens. I recalled the delightful experience of getting a dime change on each nickel I put down on the

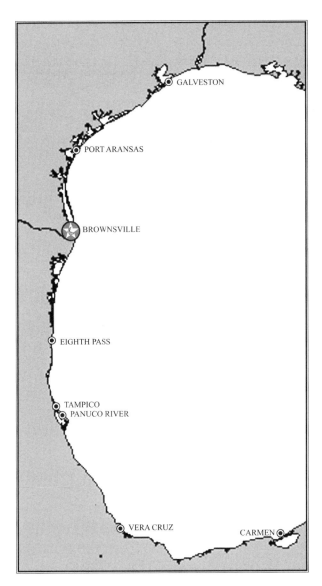

GALVESTON

PORT ARANSAS

BROWNSVILLE

EIGHTH PASS

TAMPICO
PANUCO RIVER

VERA CRUZ

CARMEN

bar for a shot of tequila. It was a little bar, far from the tourist traps, and I was the only gringo in it. Getting that dime change for a nickel seemed such a beautiful way to accumulate money that I could hardly walk out of the bar by the time I thought about the rate of exchange—four to one at that time. I realized I wasn't actually making money. But it was fun.

So was the trip to Highway Bend the next day—and as we approached it, Dave and I recalled the "sleeper" we had encountered there years before. A five-foot tarpon, a loner, lying near the bluff on which we stood—and way down deep. And he paid no attention to the lovely lures we brought right past his snout. Finally Dave got disgusted and said, "I'll wake him up," and proceeded to cast over the tarpon, bring the big plug back and drive a hook in the fish's body. He got action, all right—and a scale for a souvenir.

I have wished many times since then that we had merely waited in order to see how often the tarpon had to come up for air. I still don't know—and apparently nobody else bothers to find out.

We didn't wait.

And mentioning the sleeper brought back still another memory—the tarpon that I "walked to death," as Hurt said at the time. He sure was glad I walked it to death, for I had the doggone thing hooked on top, right back of the head, and I had to land it to keep Hurt's River Rodeo from being a disaster. I've mentioned that Hurt ran a tackle store. When he noted the spectacular achievements in the early tarpon rodeos at Port Isabel, then elsewhere on up the Texas coast, he decided to throw a River Rodeo at the mouth of the Rio Grande. He got permission to use three small boats to take anglers across the river—but only at the mouth.

Tarpon were there and they were striking, mostly right up close to the shore on the Mexican side. But anglers began wading out a little, splashing and whooping things up, and after five or six big ones had danced on out to sea carrying plugs—or mullet—the fish quit striking.

I moved on up stream a bit, looking for a traveler—a tarpon on the move. I spotted one and he hit. On the first jump he threw the plug, but it flew beyond him a bit, and when I struck I slammed it into him just back of the head and a hook took hold. A foul-hooked tarpon can be a boring creature. He won't jump, he won't make a flashy run, he just dogs it on and on, about the way a huge jewfish would.

I had barely enough line—25-pound test silk—to reach to shallow water on the far side of the river. And since the line had undoubtedly weakened to about 15-pound test near the leader, about all I could do was stay parallel with the fish. So it was back and forth, upstream, then downstream. He wouldn't go on out into the Gulf, which he could easily have done, because the wild Indians gathered there at the mouth scared him back. After an hour my hands began cramping. I was using an oversize version of an ordinary freshwater reel—no internal drag. I had to apply pressure with my thumb, or both thumbs. And they were protected by knitted stalls.

After an hour and a half I decided to clamp down and let him break loose. But I heard the buzz of an outboard motor, and here came Hurt toward me.

"Land him for me," Hurt pleaded. "Nobody has caught one yet. And the reporters and photographers . . ."

"I'll try," I said.

Two hours, and the trail I was walking, back and forth, began getting deeper. Three hours, and I couldn't take it anymore. I got a grip on the sand with my feet and clamped down with both thumbs—on the sides of the reel spool, not on that tiny bit of line left on the reel. I guess it was pretty funny, me and that tarpon doing our tug-of-war. He would thrust with his broad tail, trying to surge forward, and I would lean way over as far as I could without falling, but I wouldn't give him an inch of line. When he stopped and sighed, maybe sticking his nose up just enough to get a breath of air, I would work on him, getting back four or five feet of line.

Then another surge. The fragile, worn line held.

Finally, after a sort of token thrust, he gave up—I could turn him against his will. Once you turn the head of a big fish your way, you've got him whipped. Slowly, gently I pumped him on in. He never did turn on his side, signal of complete defeat, because I had not been able to work on him hard enough. So when his belly touched sand near shore, I made a dash at him and stuck my right hand under a gill flap. I could easily have lost him if I had let him alone, for with solid ground to help, he might have made a lunge violent enough to break the line.

As I slid him up to safety, I heard the buzz of an outboard motor. It was Hurt. He ain't no Greek, but he was bearing a gift, a noble gift. For just as I sort of sagged down on the sand, letting my tackle slide out of my hands as though I would never use it again, Hurt pitched a bottle of tequila on the beach beside me. Yes, a truly noble gesture. After three solid pulls, I took in a deep breath, like a tarpon rolling, picked up my tackle, and started looking for another traveler.

How long does it take to land a tarpon? From three seconds to three hours. Yes, I landed a tarpon, a big one, in three seconds—and at the mouth of the Rio Grande. Another memory.

He came storming at my plug just as I was getting ready to lift it out of the water, about six feet from shore. He lunged in the air the instant he slammed his jaws shut on the plug. He was pointed my way, so when I leaned into him hard—I had fairly hefty tackle that day—here he came, right out onto solid land. The plug jerked free—but I landed my tarpon.

That day, that last journey to the river where the Silver King and I were introduced, the three of us fished from one boat, which we seldom do when working tarpon holed up in a bend of a river. But Hurt had a solid 18-foot boat, quite a contrast to the 10-foot cartop rigs we had used in the past. Also we knew each other—complete confidence. It's the stranger that I dread to fish with in a small boat surrounded by tarpon.

Dave was right—they wouldn't strike. And I mean they wouldn't pay attention to plugs on top, anywhere between top and bottom, or on the bottom. All the old tricks failed.

We sat for a moment, each knowing what the others were thinking. Should we try what we called the Panuco Panic? The trick we learned years before in the Panuco—and, as you might expect, because of a backlash.

"He ought to have something to remember," Dave said to Hurt—talking about me.

"Okay," Hurt said, as he put his gear down and picked up a paddle, ready to defend himself. "Your honor."

He was talking to me. No anglers are crazy enough to have more that one lure at a time in the water when indulging in the Panuco Panic. So I let my fast-sinking lure go straight down, although as always, it didn't seem to be going straight down. Even though the rod tip was six feet from the boat, the line seemed to be slanting in right under the boat.

I gave it the works.

In the Panuco Panic, you rest the plug a moment on the bottom, right under the boat, then instead of nudging, you reel rapidly until the plug is five or six feet from the bottom. Then you pause and give one little jiggle and reel rapidly again for four or five feet. Keep doing that until you bring the lure to the surface. And as my plug neared the surface that day I saw the huge, open mouth of a tarpon right below it. He wasn't more than eight feet from me and he was staring at me as he slammed his mighty jaws shut.

I guess I got scared. Anyway, I jerked the plug out of his mouth just as he slammed his jaws shut. I refused to let him have my plug. He came on up in the air anyway. Real fine sight.

Then it was Dave's turn. He hung his tarpon, but he lost it on the first jump.

Each time we raised a tarpon, we moved the boat a little—using paddles, not the motor. There was no wind that early in the day to cause a drift.

Now it was Hurt's turn.

I knew he didn't like that sort of nonsense at all. But—it was my farewell trip. So down went his lure—and up came a tarpon. And that one, a five-footer, came arching over the little boat and fell smack in Hurt's lap.

I guess Dave and I have had more memory laughs about that than any other experience in our years of fishing together, but it was a long time before Hurt saw the humor of it. What would you do with a completely green, five-foot tarpon flailing wildly in your lap, banging a pig plug around, knocking over the tackle boxes and creating hell generally?

Well, Hurt said, "Shoo! Shoo, Tarpon!"

You'd figure he was telling a chicken to go away. And he kept making little motions with his hands as though he was going to push the tarpon over the side, yet he wouldn't touch it.

Hurt Batsell has about as much courage, physical and moral, as any man I've known. But he has always been squeamish about touching fish that are alive—or even dead ones. He'll go hungry before he cleans one.

So he was making those little gestures, without touching the fish. It finally bounced over the side and took off. Hurt grabbed his tackle just before it was jerked into the water, and, crazy as it seems, boated the tarpon. Dave carefully released it.

Then I boated one about the same size. As Dave held it with the big pliers we carry for the purpose, he said, "Want a scale for a souvenir?"

"No. Biologists say a fungus is likely to set in where the scale was pulled off," I said.

"Aw, what the hell, pollution and stopping the flow of water will kill them anyway. Have a scale on me."

He jerked off a scale, using small pliers, and handed it to me, then released the fish. Later each of us wrote his name on the scale—and the date and place. I was going to keep it. But somewhere along the line it got lost. I'm not the pack-rat type—what I specialize in keeping is memories. And that trip was a memory.

Dave landed a tarpon in a short time, then the three of us landed three more. Pretty wild fishing—and no more tarpon in the boat. And now? No more tarpon . . . well, let's talk about maybe bringing tarpon back into rivers. Hell, let's go whole hog and put them in lakes.

# CHAPTER 17

# Bring 'Em Inland

While I was writing the previous chapter about my farewell to the Rio Grande, I got to thinking about those landlocked tarpon in my resaca at Brownsville more than thirty years before. Then I was suddenly brought up short by a story in the paper about a man landing a fifteen-pound striped bass in a Texas lake.

Aha! Maybe I wasn't as much of a dreamer back in the 1930s as some people thought. Suddenly an old, discarded idea came galloping back, demanding reassessment. If they can bring the striped bass inland—and obviously they can—how about tarpon? And maybe snook? Maybe that's the way to save these fish if conditions in their home waters continue getting worse.

I called a longtime friend, Marion Toole, director of inland fisheries of the Texas Parks & Wildlife Service. Toole was in the process of clearing out his desk, getting ready to retire to the cabin he had built on a nearby lake. I hadn't seen him in several years, because I had been doing no writing about the great outdoors.

"What about those striped bass in lakes here in Texas?" I asked.

"It's for real, judging by the way things are going now," Toole said. "They're taking hold in four or five lakes in the eastern part of the state. Plenty of stripers around five and six pounds now, and occasionally one over ten pounds."[1]

"What do fishermen think when they catch one?" I asked.

"A lot of them think they're catching white bass," he said. "But they find out when they eat the fish—stripers are better."

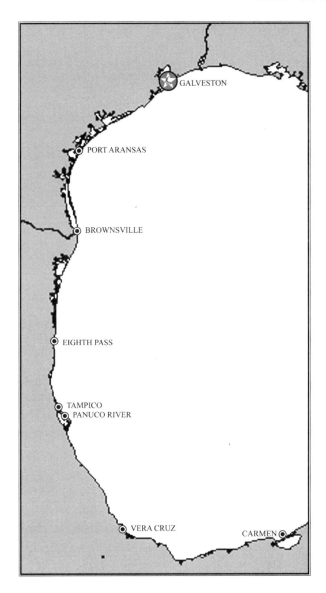

The white bass actually is a freshwater variation of striped bass—a subspecies that developed when striper were trapped up rivers now and then in the dim distant past. The fish look alike and they school up and feed and act a lot alike, one of the major differences being in size. Stripers get up to sixty pounds and more, whereas a five-pound white bass is quite unusual. Mostly they're little fellows, from two pounds down. So quite naturally an angler not in on the doings of the aquatic biologists would get bug-eyed when he caught a fifteen-pound "white bass." There ain't no such animal.

"I'm thinking now about tarpon and snook," I told Toole. "I know they get along fine in fresh, landlocked basins, but I'm wondering about reproduction. Do the stripers reproduce in lakes?"

Toole said the chances are they will never reproduce satisfactorily in lakes.

"White bass fight their way up to the headwaters of streams that flow into lakes," he said.

"How well I know," I told him. "I've had plenty of wild fishing there."

"They spawn in fast-running water, but the eggs of the white bass settle immediately to the bottom and stick like glue to rocks. They're washed by the water and hatch.

"Not the same with stripers. They spawn in rivers, all right. But they need flotation for the eggs—must float, between bottom and top of a flowing stream, for two or three days before they hatch.

"You don't find much of that kind of water in the streams that keep our lakes full."

"So what do you do?" I asked.

"Do their lovemaking for them, the same as biologists have been doing with rainbow trout and some other fish for years," Toole said. "We got our first small stripers from hatcheries in Virginia and the Carolinas. But we've already learned to hand-raise the fish—to milk the female and get the eggs, then milk the male and get a deposit of sperm on the eggs to fertilize them.

"We've got stripers of our own big enough, around five pounds, to spawn. So we're set."

In a way, the story of the white bass and the story of the striped bass just about mark the beginning and the end of Toole's long career as an aquatic biologist with the Texas Parks and Wildlife Service. For he was on hand when white bass were spread across Texas—the originals having been taken from Caddo Lake, on the Texas–Louisiana line. Now most lakes, big and small, in Texas are lousy with white bass. Too many of them, as proved by the puny size of those usually caught, in sharp contrast to the whoppers, around three to five pounds, that were common when the lakes were new and white bass had just been put in them.

There is no need to raise white bass in hatcheries, since one female spawns maybe a couple of hundred thousand eggs, depending on her size, in sharp contrast to eight thousand or so eggs spawned by a female black bass.

But stripers—different story there. As Toole said, man will have to carry out their sex life for them.

And so I said to Toole, "Well, how about my tarpon and snook?"

"You'll have to find out from somebody else," Toole said. "You know where my work has been done—in freshwater and with freshwater fish."

"Thanks," I said. "I'll find out."

I just thought I would. Evidently nobody in a position to do anything about it—no marine biologists or anybody else—has even thought of bringing these great game fish inland and planting them. And, of course, nobody has considered milking these fish at hatcheries and getting fertile eggs and young the way biologists have been doing with rainbow trout and a few other species for years, and the way they're now doing with striped bass. And when I meditate on the probable reaction of a five-foot lady tarpon when some guy undertakes to milk her, I can understand why no biologist has given serious thought to such an undertaking.[2]

Want to try milking a wildcat?

In a final comment that day, Toole told me that it now appears that the newly introduced striped bass may prove the salvation of many of our lakes which are being ruined by the gizzard shad. The shad are more numerous than the predatory fish and grow faster. They get so big, two or three pounds, that black bass and white bass can't eat them. So they take over. Toole thinks the stripers may bring about an adjustment in that situation in a hurry. They love gizzard shad—and a fifteen-pounder can take on any gizzard shad alive. All very nice—except that some flaws in the current pattern of thinking about this situation are likely to be revealed eventually. Big striped bass may prefer black bass to gizzard shad.

Then what?

Anyway, I took off on my search, and it can rightly be called a search instead of research. I wanted to find somebody who knew enough about tarpon and snook to at least discuss the possibility of planting these fish inland.

I didn't find anybody.

So I speculate and draw dream pictures that some biologist may fill out later if tarpon are on the way out as a result of the manner in which man has managed and mismanaged his environment. And I don't pour it on anybody—not even Modern Man specifically. After all, man began wrecking the environment when he learned to cultivate crops eight thousand or more years ago. We're just speeding up the process of wrecking.

But we know what we are doing. Maybe we can "turn back" in some ways? I figure we may not do so in time to save tarpon, since all those marine hatchery experiments along our coasts are concerned with eating fish—redfish, speckled trout, flounder, even shrimp—and not tarpon. So let's take a look.

Right off the bat I suggest that somebody get busy and put hundreds of thousands of baby tarpon and snook in the big lakes in the far southern part of Texas, where chances of the fish surviving during winter will be best. Getting the tiny fish wouldn't be much of a job. Just nose around the coastal area of the southern part of Mexico for a month or so and find the hideouts of the babies, then catch them in nets, put them in tanks, and fly them to Texas. And, in the process, fly plenty of them to big lakes in Mexico, if the Mexican government wants that.

The cost would be trivial compared to what we spend in raising catfish and bass in hatcheries. And there is absolutely no doubt about tarpon and snook thriving in such fresh waters, at least for a time, for both species—maybe some stay there. Nobody knows.

In Texas the stocking program might well be started at Falcon Lake, southeast of Laredo on the Rio Grande. That's warm country. Sure, the snook—and probably tarpon also—in my resaca died when the temperature dropped to around twenty and stayed there three days. But my resaca is only twelve feet at its deepest spot, whereas Falcon Lake is more than two hundred feet deep near the dam. There's a big difference. No cold wave is going to lower the temperature of that water enough to hurt tarpon or snook.

The still larger and brand new Amistad Lake farther up the Rio Grande (near the town of Del Rio) would be another fine spot for some planting. The program might include stocking these fish in lakes still farther north in Texas—Lake Corpus Christi, the Hill Country lakes near Austin, the lakes from Houston on north for two hundred miles or so. And the argument I used to get—that tarpon might kill out the bass—is no longer tenable in view of those striped bass being stocked in Texas lakes.

And what the hell? Suppose tarpon did kill out a lot of bass? It's a simple job to replace them from hatcheries, and hanging a five-foot tarpon in, let's say, Lake Travis, near Austin, would be an event in a fisherman's life that no bass take of any kind could ever match.

There are at least twenty-five large lakes and about a hundred smaller ones in Texas that are deep enough to offer a chance for survival of tarpon, especially since it seldom stays cold more than three or four days anywhere in Texas except the extreme western part and the Panhandle. As for the Panhandle—"Gee, I'll bet it's cold at Amarillo," the man said as he stood at the North Pole. Would the fish reproduce? Probably not—at least I doubt very much if tarpon would, for it seems obvious that those dopey larval forms must fiddle around in offshore Gulf or Atlantic Ocean waters for a spell before moving to shore and becoming true fish and carrying on.

Snook might. I've heard dozens of reports about landing snook in various lakes in Mexico and Central America. Tex Purvis, who has operated a guide service in Mexico, says tarpon remain year-round in a landlocked lake up the Usamacinta River, which is at the border of Mexico and Guatemala. I've fished near the river, which empties into the Gulf of Campeche just west of Carmen. But I've never been up it—and I've never heard of any landlocked lake up the river.

The same goes for Lake Nicaragua. Tarpon are so numerous there that native fishermen working in the river below the lake always keep a paddle handy to defend themselves against leaping tarpon. But Lake Nicaragua is not landlocked—and I don't think any lake up the Usamacinta River is landlocked. People think they are. But contact between lake and saltwater is always made during periods of heavy rain. In fact, I think snook crossed the narrow land barrier between oceans by storming out of such lakes in both directions during periods of tremendous rainfall. They had to make contact some way, and if you have a better theory, haul it out and defend it.

Well, what do we do if they won't reproduce in our lakes?

It's simplifying the situation to say that we will continue seining small snook and tarpon out of waters south of the Rio Grande and flying the fish to our lakes. For we are ignoring the possibility that there may not be any small tarpon down there to catch. So how about raising tarpon in hatcheries, as I mentioned? It might work—it might not. That mighty female, and her male boyfriend, could conceivably be quieted down with a shot of the stuff they use to put big game animals to sleep temporarily. Then they could be handled. Or could we build on the coast a hatchery where the tarpon could be confined and might do their own mating without help?

Nobody knows. Nobody seems to care.

Latest information I have is that the saltwater hatcheries don't seem to be doing much good in restocking the bays with redfish and speckled trout, although the work is being continued. Also more and more redfish are being stocked in lakes in west Texas, where there is considerable salinity in the water. Reds are caught there now and then, but there is no evidence of reproduction.[3]

But tarpon and particularly snook are different—they go up rivers; redfish and speckled trout and flounder don't. It might turn out to be easier to arrange an environment in which tarpon and snook will reproduce—and in which the young, even those larval tarpon, can be nursed along until they're big enough to be planted in a lake. That's going to be an interesting biological experiment, if it is ever made—that larval tarpon. What does he feed on? Can his natural food be duplicated? And is there any reason why we don't find out?

Snook should be an easy species to deal with, for they reach maturity around six pounds—about the same as striped bass—and can even be milked even if they don't like it. And real fish, not larvae, hatch out of the eggs.

If we don't make a genuine effort to bring these two great game fish, one of which is finer eating that any freshwater fish, inland, then we are passing up a really great opportunity. There is no way of knowing just how far north tarpon and snook might survive, if the water is deep. And if it's too cold, heat the doggone stuff. Plenty of water in lakes, mostly man-made, near every industrial plant is heated. Tarpon and snook might very well make it through the winter huddling around the hot water coming out of such plants.

Bass lead a lazy, luxurious life in Lake Calavaras, which is heated by water coming out of the power plant that supplies San Antonio and surrounding area. Why wouldn't tarpon love it there? And at similar plants scattered all over the country?

We just haven't bothered to consider such a possibility. We spend millions of dollars restocking lakes with catfish—which you can have. But we won't even spend a hundred thousand to lug some baby tarpon and snook from Mexico to Texas and see how they do in our lakes.

It's time somebody did something.

I'll move on now to that final chapter—a discussion of what we might do to help the tarpon in his natural environment.

# CHAPTER 18

# Where Do We Go Now?

And so we come to the Big Question: Should the title of this book be *Decline and Fall of the Silver King*? Or is there a chance we might check the decline—maybe even give the tarpon a nudge upward? What man hath wrought, man may not be able to "unwrought." And if you can't find that word "unwrought" in your dictionary, put it there. It's a good word. But man can try.

If you bear in mind that any good things we do for those estuarine creatures that are of commercial value—redfish, flounder, speckled trout, croakers, shrimp, and so on—are almost certain to bring an equal benefit to tarpon, then you might start hoping. The first thing we must do is to admit that tarpon fishing is shot to hell—that tarpon in the Gulf of Mexico all the way down to Vera Cruz are coming upon hard times. Before you can cure an illness, you must admit it and diagnose it. We refuse to do that about our coastal fishing because doing so may be bad for the tourist business.

Just to prove the point, I wrote several chambers of commerce along the Texas coast asking about tarpon fishing. One or two ignored my letter—they smelled something because they remembered outdoor columns of mine in Texas newspapers that told about the decline of the tarpon. But from Port Isabel, my old stomping (not stamping) ground, I got a cheery letter saying tarpon fishing was fine and come on down.

How fine?

I've mentioned that in the 1971 annual fishing roundup (once called tarpon rodeo) at Port Isabel, one eighteen-inch tarpon was caught. Tarpon

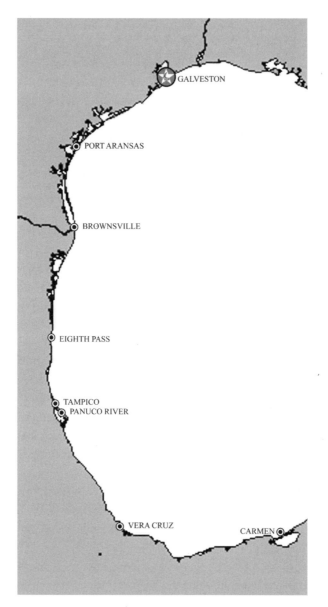

fishing is fine? But the speckled trout situation is obviously not much better. Remember that two-and-a-half-pound speck that won top prize in the
same fishing rodeo? The big trout of earlier days would have swallowed
him. It's the same way all along the Texas coast.

In three years only two small tarpon were caught in the Freeport fishing
rodeo—which was also a tarpon rodeo in earlier days. And those small

fish were caught by anglers trolling for Spanish mackerel. Nobody really fished for tarpon.

Tarpon are practically gone from the New Brazos. I've told about the Rio Grande. I did a lot of checking all along the coast, but I had to go to newspaper outdoor writers to get the truth, and I promised that I would not identify them. They must write only "constructive" stuff about fishing. Instead of saying that anglers catch a wad of baby trout—a half a pound each—at times these writers use the term "school trout." Any time you see that, you can be certain the trout are in the nine- to twelve-inch range—half a pound or less.

It's more fun dipping goldfish out of a bowl.

Not only is the term "school trout" a euphemism, as used here, it is really inaccurate. For practically all speckled trout are "school fish," except during the spawning season. And quite obviously they get back together, in schools, after spawning, as demonstrated by the great schools of five- to ten-pound trout we once encountered in the Eighth Pass in Mexico. But when you read in Texas newspapers about school trout, you can know they are babies.

A snook is a rarity on the Texas coast. Now and then anglers will get into a school of fair-sized redfish, but mostly they catch what we used to call rat reds—two pounds or so.

Okay, tarpon have almost disappeared from the Texas coast. How about Mexico?

I haven't been there in a long time, so I called Dave Young at Brownsville.

"I went to the Panuco," he said. "Couldn't believe it—no tarpon. Not even any mullet. People told me that a huge cotton acreage has developed up the river and that the stuff is being saturated with pesticides."

"You hear anything about Carmen?" I asked.

"Now and then I see somebody's that been there," Dave said. "But if I ask about tarpon, they seem surprised."

"Progress," as we understand that term, is moving south, bringing untold "blessings" to those so-called underdeveloped countries.

And when Mexicans get heptachlor and dieldrin and endrin, they're just as wild with the stuff as they were with airplanes when they first started work as commercial airline pilots. I know—I flew with them. It was a game to them.

How about Florida? And the West Indies? And Guatemala?

I don't need to find out. As that editor once told a writer who complained that his whole story was not read, "It is not necessary to eat all of an egg to find out if it is rotten." You look at what's happened on the Texas coast and you know what's happened or is beginning to happen throughout the entire range of tarpon.

I know it may sound absurd to speculate on the extinction of the tarpon, since one female lays 12 million eggs and you can find tarpon by the thousands at many spots—probably including Carmen. But there is a vast difference in the critical number that signals an endangered species. It may be several million tarpon but only a few thousand whitetail deer.

Bear in mind that the passenger pigeon was not killed out by man with a gun. He vanished almost overnight when destruction of his nesting areas and roosts suddenly reduced his numbers to, let's say, a mere million or so. Crowding means different things to different species.

The coyote continues increasing, both in range and numbers, in spite of trapping and poisoning. But the plains wolf vanished from Texas. Man "crowded" him—the coyote doesn't mind being crowded. In a way, he likes it. If he is deprived of rabbits and rats and man's sheep, he eats man's watermelons and cucumbers and cantaloupes. He is adaptable. The wolf was not. And the tarpon is not.

So it is conceivable that he could vanish, at least from vast areas of the Gulf coast, almost overnight. He might reach a point where young, including those dopey larvae, can't stand up under the pressure of normal predators—and bingo! He's gone.

I say this is possible. I'm not predicting it—I choose to hope, even though doing so may be indulging in dreams. But I do know that before we can do anything to save him, assuming that we want to, we must admit the sorry state of tarpon today. And that of other estuarine creatures.

Then as my No. 2 suggestion, I recommend that somebody get busy and find out about the life cycle of the tarpon. And nobody really knows. I'm not expressing my opinion alone—I quote from "on high." I have a letter from A. N. Woodall, assistant chief of the Division of Fishery Research of the U.S. Fish and Wildlife Service, about this.

Woodall's letter starts:

"Since receiving your interesting letter about the tarpon, I have been searching for an 'expert' to help answer your questions. I've come to the conclusion that tarpon experts are as scarce as tarpon."

So there you have your "official" verification of my statement.

My No. 3 suggestion is that all pesticides of the chlorinated hydrocarbon group—the everlasting killers—be banished from the land.

My No. 4 suggestion is that all other forms of pollution in our rivers be stopped—and stopped now.

My No. 5 suggestion is that the industrial plants that kill all plankton in water used to cool the plants be forced to put the plankton back—or run a plankton-bearing channel around the plant. It's stupid to brag about releasing chemically pure water from an industrial plant if the water is biologically dead.

My No. 6 suggestion is that all commercial fishing and shrimping in all our shore waters—and for five miles out to sea—be banned entirely. Sure redfish and speckled trout are fine eating. But did you ever consider this: The total catch of these fish for a year would not feed the people of Houston for one day. Yet we stand by and watch a fine sports fishery destroyed because the people on the coast will not admit the truth—bad publicity— and because most of the state representatives from the coastal area are on retainers by the fish and shrimp operators. They block all attempts at conservation. I'm quite familiar with that story, for I've appeared several times before legislative committees considering conservation bills—and each time I knew that a majority of the members were on retainers from the fish and shrimp operators. So the fishing goes to hell.

And the outdoor writer must talk about "school trout," instead of about baby trout. And he does not say that there are not enough tarpon to justify a trip because he is instructed not to say that. I'm not going way out of the way to pour it on anybody. It just happens that several outdoor writers for papers in coastal cities have told me what the situation is . . . and they can't tell it in print. They'd like to pour it on. They aren't permitted to do so.

Suggestion No. 7 is this: Force those who control the flow of our rivers to permit a small but steady flow into saltwater where there was such a flow before man started building dams. It's actually criminal to kill the Rio Grande—to cut flow entirely and watch a bar form across the mouth of the stream. It's tragic that water near the mouth of the Brazos moves back and forth with the tide—no flow.

That's just the beginning. Unless there is a change, the mighty Mississippi may stop flowing to the sea.

You think I'm kidding? Go look at plans for "water development and multiuse," as it is called, for the Mississippi. There is even a plan to take water out of it and run the stuff by canal all the way across Texas to the Rio

Grande. Man can stop the flow of the mighty river into the Gulf. And history tells us that what man can do, he is very likely to do. The Bomb, for example.

There are many other things that should be done. For example, checking the conversion of bay shores into housing projects. As Dr. Carl Hubbs, professor of zoology at the University of Texas told me. "In building marinas on bays, we may be defeating the purposes of them," he said.

That is, we build marinas so fishermen can relax in comfort on the water and storm out in a hurry in a fast boat and get into the action—tarpon, trout, reds. And they usually return with limp spirits and maybe a batch of baby trout and hardhead catfish—turd rustlers, as we who know fishing call them. The turd rustler loves to be "crowded" by man. He swarms under the overwater toilets and gorges on human feces.

But tarpon and trout and redfish? Maybe such crowding doesn't kill them—it merely drives them away, and they find a home in some other bay. Then man follows them to that bay and starts building more marinas
. . .

When will we run out of bays? An interesting question.

I wind up this dissertation with a prediction that the silver king will survive, at least in a considerable part of his vast range. I know he will survive if enough people learn the truth and start acting on the basis of what they learn.

So I conclude by repeating the opening comment in this book: Dedicated to the proposition that the tarpon shall not vanish from the seas.

May the "Glory of the Silver King" shine on.

# Endnotes

PROLOGUE: AND IN THE BEGINNING . . .

1. Stilwell wrote *Glory of the Silver King* at the infancy of tarpon and snook research. In fact, he chronicles his search for reliable biological research in Chapter 17. The information Stilwell presents here was the accepted biology of the time and may not be as accurate as our information today. For the most accurate and up-to-date tarpon research, please visit www.bonefishandtarpon.org.

2. *Rube Goldberg*, ed. Lorraine Kennedy, May 2002, Rube Goldberg, Inc., Westport, Connecticut (www.rubegoldberg.com). Reuben Lucius Goldberg was an inventor, Pulitzer Prize–winning cartoonist, sculptor, and author. Rube Goldberg is best known for his complex "inventions," and in this twisted, neogolistic world, he has become an adjective. The *Webster's New World Dictionary* describes a Rube Goldberg as "a comically involved, complicated invention, laboriously contrived to perform a simple operation."

3. The speckled sea trout, *Cynscion nebulosus*, is often referred to as a weakfish; however, it is not. The weakfish, *Cynoscion regalis*, is a close relative, but prefers the cool waters of the Atlantic. The natural range of the weakfish is from northern Florida to Nova Scotia. Although both fish are called trout, they are not true trout members of the family Salmonidae.

4. For more information on Stilwell's journeys into Mexico, read his seminal account of fishing in Mexico in the 1948 *Fishing in Mexico*, published by Alfred A. Knopf. The book is currently out of print; however, it is still available secondhand on Amazon .com.

5. Although Stilwell never published *Glory of the Silver King*, tarpon aficionados, conservation associations, concerned biologists, and recreational fishing clubs have made tarpon one of the most respected and protected fish species in the Gulf of Mexico. The sheer reverence that Hart felt for these ancient fish is shared by anglers around the world, and it has contributed to their healthy population return.

For more information on tarpon and snook research and conservation, please visit www.tarpontomorrow.org and www.snookfoundation.org.

CHAPTER 1: THE SPORT OF PRESIDENTS

1. "History," *The Historic Queen Isabel Inn*, ed. Mike Cox, June 2001, Port Isabel, Texas, www.queenisabelinn.com/history.html. The hotel served as a focal point for President-Elect Warren G. Harding's vacation in November 1920. The hotel was also the birthplace and headquarters for the Rio Grande Valley Fishing Rodeo. The rodeo, started in 1934 by the hotel's manager, Dr. J. A. Hockaday, would later become the Texas International Fishing Tournament (TIFT), which is still in existence today.

2. Evan Anders, *Boss Rule in South Texas*, Austin, University of Texas Press, 1982. Rentfro Banton Creager (1877–1950) was a Brownsville political boss in early twentieth-century politics in Brownsville. He began his political arc as an attorney turned Customs Collector in the tumultuous border feuds of the 1920s. As Republican political boss, he was offered the ambassadorship to Mexico twice, once by President Harding and again by President Coolidge; he declined both offers. There is strong circumstantial evidence that Stilwell based *Border City*'s (Doubleday, Doran and Company, Inc., 1945) antagonistic character, Jim Billings, on R. B. Creager.

3. Stilwell was writing *Glory of the Silver King* nearly fifty years after the events occurred. President Harding's vacation started in November. This would have made the tarpon he fished for late season fish. The typical Texas tarpon season ranges from May until late October, with a few larger fish remaining into late December.

4. FDR did, in fact, catch a few tarpon while staying at the famed Port Aransas, Texas, Tarpon Inn in 1937. For a full account of FDR's Port Aransas visit, read Barney Farley's *Fishing Yesterday's Gulf Coast*, Texas A&M University Press, 2002.

5. Stilwell's original manuscript read: "A Farewell to Arms, or maybe Bells . . ." However, for readers who may not be familiar with Ernest Hemingway's work the editor added the full title, *For Whom the Bell Tolls*.

CHAPTER 3: KING OF TARPON RIVERS

1. Harry Sedgwick caught the 247-pound International Gamefish Association World Record on 24 March 1938 on the Panuco River, using 130-pound test line. Information courtesy of Jason Schratweiser, International Game Fish Association.

2. "Dama comenzo historia del TIPS," Milenio.com, ed. Francisco Pineda and Pedro Elizalde Sigala, 8 June 2009, Tampico, Mexico, www.milenio.com/node/262591. The Tampico Tarpon Rodeo is Stilwell's name for the International Fishing Tournament Tarpon that was organized by Bueron Maria Barcena of the Club de Regatas

Corona. The event, first held in 1942, was organized to mimic tarpon rodeos held in the United States. In fact, Leroy H. Dorsey, founder of the Southwest Pass Tarpon Rodeo in New Orleans, Louisiana, helped Barcena organize the first Tampico rodeo on 17 March 1942. The rodeo is still in existence, and it is one of the oldest, continuous tarpon rodeos held in the Gulf of Mexico.

3. The official tournament archives state that only twenty-five anglers participated in the first rodeo; however, Stilwell may be counting anglers who actually caught tarpon over five feet and entered them into the rodeo.

CHAPTER 4: NOBLE EXPERIMENTS

1. Besides his alcoholism, Stilwell had a special affinity for women. His misogyny toward women is well documented in *Border City* (Doubleday, Doran and Company, Inc., 1945) and *Campus Town* (Doubleday, Doran and Company, Inc., 1950). *Campus Town*, in fact, is better remembered for the Rudolph Belarski cover painting of a buxom blonde in a torn red dress in the throes of a ravaging group of Ku Klux Klan members than for its plot. Stilwell, married twice, divorced his first wife of thirty years, Mary Gray Seabury, in 1955 and married Anne Elizabeth Stone twenty-six days later, to whom he remained married for the rest of his life.

2. Hart Stilwell's *Border City* and Americo Paredes's *George Washington Gomez* (Arte Publico Press, 1990) both have an Anglo character who plays an important and heroic role in the first Brownsville Charro Days. The character is an Anglo but owns the Brownsville Spanish language theatre. The evidence is too compelling not to think it is Dave Young.

CHAPTER 6: THE TRUE BELIEVER

1. Eric Hoffer, *The True Believer: Thoughts on the Nature of Mass Movements*, New York, Harper & Row, 1951. Hoffer's general thesis states that fanatics will switch between mass movements that still have the basic tenets of their beliefs intact. In Hurt's case, he was a die-hard topwater tarpon fan, which most anglers are, but to catch tarpon he was willing to switch from the tried-and-true method of top-fishing to follow the mass movement and bottom-fish with Dave and Hart.

CHAPTER 7: CONQUEST OF THE PANUCO

1. The practice of moving into another angler's fishing hole is commonly referred to as "potlicking." Although Stilwell takes a fairly lackadaisical approach to it here, the practice today is extremely frowned upon and can lead to boat ramming;

casting lures at each other; and, in excessive cases, brawls. Moreover, from a law enforcement standpoint, this practice maybe construed as herding or harassing fish.

CHAPTER 8: BAY OF THE IGUANAS

1. The original manuscript read:

   Times sure change. Once there was a saying among archaeologists that you could go to the remotest corner of the earth to start a new dig and find a message from some "Humperdink." German archaeologists did a lot of pioneering.

   The passage was removed because the reference to "Humperdink" was too vague.
2. Brandon Shuler, "Robalo on the Border," *Shallow Water Angler*, Oct.–Nov. 2007, p. 31. The current official International Game Fish Association's world record snook is listed at 53 pounds, 10 ounces, and was landed in Costa Rica. However, Texas Parks and Wildlife Department lists a 56-pound snook caught in Corpus Christi, near the present day Packery Channel, by commercial fisherman Louis Rawalt.
3. Hart Stilwell, *Fishing in Mexico*, New York, Alfred A. Knopf, 1948.
4. Mark Kurlansky, *Cod*, New York, Penguin Books, 1997. Indeed, the dish they ate was not the bacalao made from the codfish. The cod, *Gadus morhua*, was a popular Atlantic food source; however, unmitigated fishery management has led to closed fisheries on most of the east coast, from Greenland to the Carolina Outer Banks. For an excellent history on the cod fishery, read Mark Kurlansky's *Cod*.
5. Stilwell's original manuscripts read "weakfish"; however, for biological integrity the editor changed the weakfish designation to speckled trout.

CHAPTER 9: NEW BAY—CRAZY FISH

1. Stilwell is referring to the Texas International Fishing Tournament, the longest consecutive running and largest fishing tournament in Texas. The TIFT is still one of the most popular international saltwater tournaments in the nation.
2. The book Stilwell refers to is *Good Shot: A Book of Rod, Gun, and Camera*, by Bob, Dan, and Ray Holland, New York: Alfred A. Knopf, 1946.

CHAPTER 10: THE LAMPS OF MEXICO

1. The original manuscripts had a number of versions of this sentence. The editor restructured the sentence from three of the manuscripts for clarity.

2. Melville J. Herskovitz founded Northwestern University's Anthropology Department in 1938. He is best remembered for his studies on the effects of British Colonialism on the African continent. He argued that the intersections of cultures created "cultural accidents," which changed the cultural history and course of indigenous populations. He also dedicated his life's work to "cultural relativism," proposing race is sociological, not biological. In fact, in a letter dated 13 December 1948 to J. Frank Dobie, Stilwell writes:

> I have recently been doing a lot of reading of anthropology, and the question always arises as to whether a people is benefited or injured by various contacts with other peoples. I have wondered many times at the question. Do we hurt or help people such as the Mexicans when we take to them certain phases of our own culture? I know we complicate their lives and add conflict.

CHAPTER 11: THE LITTLE CHILDREN AT PLAY

1. The original draft had "featherweight" typed, then scratched out. The second draft had "featherweight" handwritten back into the draft. Although Stilwell showed reluctance to add "featherweight," the editor included the word to describe the lightweight tackle one would use to increase the sport of the catch.
2. This chapter in the most complete manuscript was apparently in the editing process at the time of Stilwell's death. This sentence in Stilwell's manuscript was scratched out and had a handwritten note above it. Some of the writing was illegible; however, the editor believes this was the sentence Stilwell intended.

CHAPTER 14: ROLLERS ON THE ROCKS

1. See Barney Farley's *Fishing Yesterday's Gulf Coast*, College Station, Texas A&M University Press, 2008.

CHAPTER 16: FAREWELL TO THE RIO GRANDE

1. Cabrito is a Mexican dish of young, milk-fed goat analogous to its beef counterpart, veal.

CHAPTER 17: BRING 'EM INLAND

1. The striper has firmly established itself in the pantheon of Texas fisheries; however, they only successfully reproduce in Lake Texoma on the Texas–Oklahoma border.

The fishery, for the most part, is a put-and-take fishery. The Texas state record as of 2009 was fifty-three pounds caught by Ron Venerable in the Brazos River.

2. As of 2009, tarpon, although extensive efforts have been made, have not spawned in captivity.

3. The Texas Parks & Wildlife Department's Coastal Fisheries Enhancement Division's redfish, speckled trout, and flounder stocking programs have become the model for coastal fisheries management. Ironically, the stocking programs were funded and supported by Dow Chemical company. The first Texas hatchery, the CCA/CPL Hatchery Unit in Corpus Christi, was funded by a gracious Coastal Conservation Association grant. As of 2009, the TPWD fisheries enhancement division has 100 percent mapped the redfish genome and can track a stocked fish's parentage down to the hatchery tank in which it was spawned.

# Index

## OTHER TITLES IN THE GULF COAST BOOKS SERIES